My Ninety Year Journey

Sharing Wisdom and Knowledge for Family Success

Owen Lee Nelson

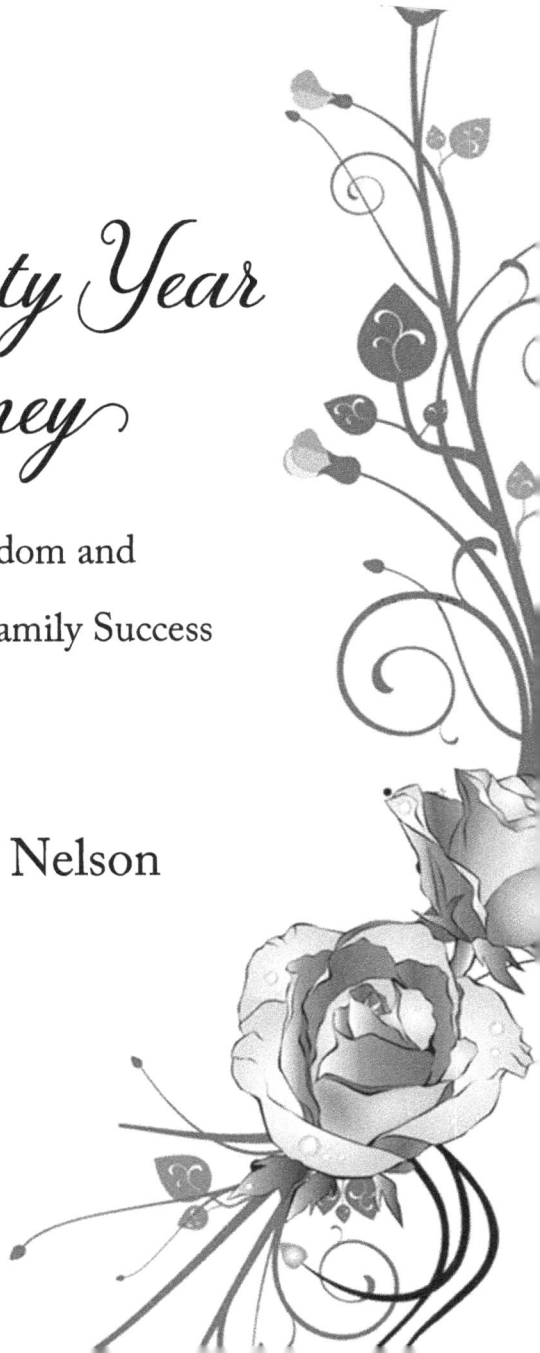

Professional Publishing House, LLC
1425 W. Manchester Avenue Suite B
Los Angeles, California 90047
323-750-3592
Email: professionalpublishinghouse@yahoo.com
www.Professionalpublishinghouse.com

First printing October 2018
978-1-7328982-0-2
10987654321

All Bible Scriptures are from the King James Version

For inquiries contact: professionalpublishinghouse@yahoo.com

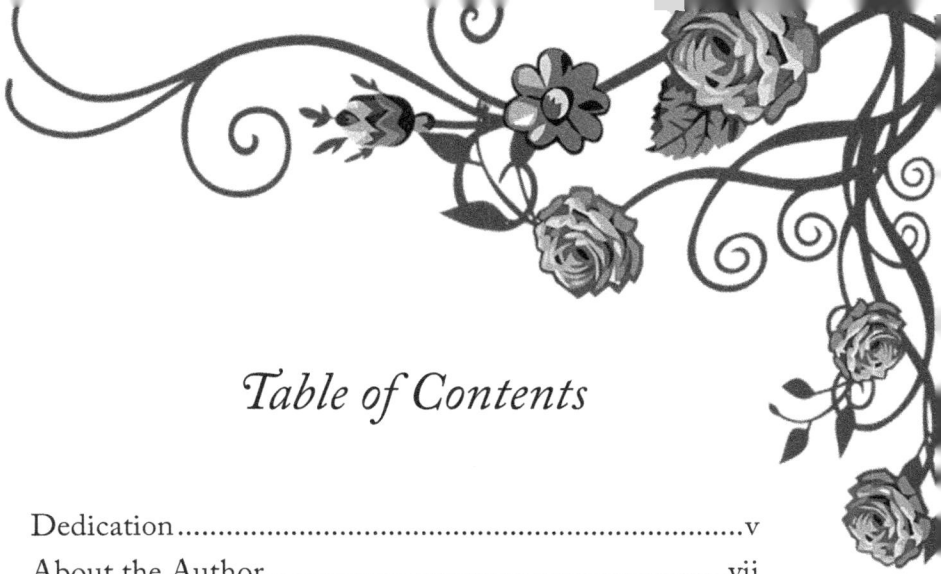

Table of Contents

Dedication

I dedicate this book to the memory of my late father, Simon Hunter, and my late mother, Florine Hunter, who were the parents of eleven children—who were dedicated to their children and worked hard to see that they had the best chance for success in life. They were also committed to their "marital vows, of staying together to death do us part." Our mother departed this life at the age of forty four.

I dedicate this also to my late Step-Mother, Lena Jennings Hunter, who later married our father, and kept the same vows, they were also separated by the call of God. Our parents are sadly missed, but my greatest comfort is knowing that they went to be with our Lord and Savior Jesus Christ.

I thank our parents for their teaching and discipline in our lives, and the things they taught us, which still resonate in our hearts today. Thanks to God, for giving us to parents who stayed with us, "trained us up" and took care of all of us to the end. (Proverbs 22:6)

About the Author

Owen Lee Nelson, the second born child to my mother, Florine Hunter, and my Father Simon Owen Hunter. I was given the name Owen after my father. I was the second child born, the first child was a girl. Although I never discussed it with my parents, I have always thought that they were planning for a boy, and the name was already planned, for their second-born child, so they gave it to me.

I never thought anything about my name until I became an adult and started working in public places and taking care of business, cashing checks, and going to doctor's offices. When my name was called, and I stood up, everyone in the area looked astonished, and whenever I had to cash a check they would say, "Your husband will have to sign." I tell you this so that when you read this book, you won't be surprised.

I was born and grew up in Como, Mississippi with my parents. They were my first teachers who taught me the basics, love, obedience, and about the only true and living God, who is our Creator. I grew up as any other child, exploring and experiencing life, learning about the good, the bad, and the ugly at a very young age. I learned right from wrong and learned my limitations within my surroundings.

As a born again Christian, I served in the church, "the Lord's House" as a Sunday school teacher, a teacher in Christian Education, Missionary teacher and leader, and as youth and adult choir director. I have attended many Christian growth sessions, and attended Midwest Bible College in Danville, Illinois receiving a Certificate in Evangelistic and Church Mission Work and the work of Christ Jesus. I also serve as a Church mother.

I have held and led many bible studies and prayer meetings in my home and neighborhood as well as community planning meetings for outreaches to children and youth.

My education has been through several academies, Southern University, Eastern University, University of Illinois, and public state training in institution food service and business management. I hold an Associate Degree in Applied Science and am a certified Dietetic Technician.

I attended the police academy in Springfield, Illinois and I received a diploma in sewing and dress making through a correspondence course from the Career Institute in Washington, DC. I took a cake decorating class at Danville Community College and learned to make wedding cakes of any size and cakes for all occasions. I have had the honor of making wedding cakes for all of my granddaughters, nieces and nephews, as well as for many non-family members, both

Black and White. I have taken courses in upholstery, early childhood development and foster care. I was appointed Surrogate Mother of Classroom by the Secretary of State and was certified as a teacher's aide in District 118.

I have worked for several businesses: Wolford Hotel, Lakeview Hospital, and Vermilion County Nursing Home. At the Vermilion County Head Start, I served as Nutritionist/ Dietetic Technician for eighteen years in Danville, Rantoul, and Champaign Counties. I also taught one semester at VOCTECH Training Center for High School students in food preparation and sanitation. I also worked for Hoopeston Migrant Center Food Services. I learned two words of their language, "see" and "chicken". Also, I organized a 4H group in the community, teaching children how to plant and harvest gardens, cook, plant flowers, sewing, about sanitation; and we went on many field trips to businesses.

This is just a few of the experiences that I have encountered, and at the age of 90 years, this is my first published book.

My Family Photos and
Fun Memories

My late husband Tom Nelson and me, Owen Nelson

Owen Nelson

Owen Nelson
at age 54

My mother
Florine Mitchell-Hunter

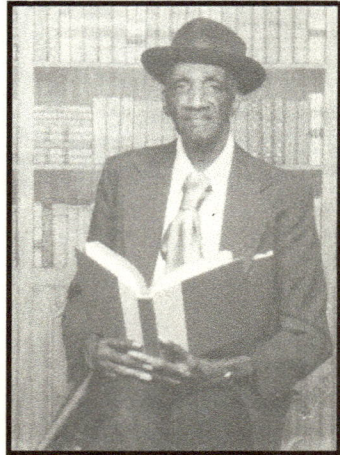

My father
Simon Owen Hunter

Oldest sister
Cora Lee Hunter

My second son
Robert Nelson

My first born
Rufus Nelson

My oldest brother, Robert Earl Hunter in his plane

Me, my brother and sisters

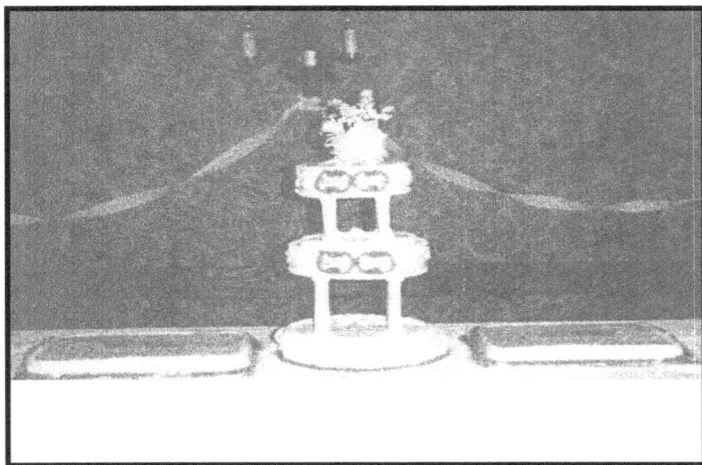

Cakes that I prepared for weddings

Home Life

My life story—The thing I remember most about growing up as a child in Mississippi is my mother and father, and my sisters and brothers. I remember my mother cooking and feeding us, and the bed we slept in. Me and my oldest sister playing with our paper dolls and the clothing for them that we cut out of a catalogue from which our parents ordered clothes for the family. When the catalogues were outdated, mother would give them to us to cut out pictures which we used for our doll house. We cut out furniture, and assembled it in one corner of the room where we slept. We found other books with animals that we used for our pasture and farms, and automobiles which we dreamed we would own one day.

Our only transportation then was the wagon and buggy that was pulled by mules and horses. I remember our father leaving our house early in the morning, and coming back later in the day, most of the time riding on the back of a mule or horse. He would tie the animal with a rope to a tree, or the post on the end of the porch until he was ready to leave again. When he got on the horse to leave again, my oldest sister, Cora Lee, and I would wave goodbye to him. We wouldn't see him again until late in the evening, even if we were in bed. As children who didn't know much about danger and trouble, but we couldn't fall sleep until we heard our father's voice. (I believe most children feel fear when their parents are not with them.)

There were eleven children born to our parents: seven girls and four boys. Two boys died as babies, and our oldest sister Cora Lee died at the age of twenty-one.

We lived in a two-bedroom house. The girls slept in one room. The boys were the youngest and slept in the room with our parents. As the boys got older, our father bought a roll away bed and built a divider wall in the kitchen for them.

We lived on our grandfather's land. Our grandfather was a slave. He inherited one hundred and sixty acres of land when the slave master died. My grandfather, Allen Hunter and Grandmother Luevenia had eight children: five sons and three daughters. He gave each of them a house on the land (the place). Each house was about a block apart. My grandfather, Allen Hunter, and his wife Luevenia lived in the big house in the center.

It was a large beautiful house. It was a bi-level with a porch on both levels with concentered pillar posts. There were beautiful flowers of all kinds. There was a fenced-in garden outside of the yard with many different kinds of vegetables. On the south side of the home was a large fruit orchard: apples, plums, grapes, peaches, berries and pears.

There was a large cedar grove with a well, a large fishing pond, and all the trees were cedar (ever greens), in which the fowls grazed. There were all sorts of fowls, chickens, geese, ducks, and guineas. (Guineas are original fowls endemic to Africa). There was a large pasture where the animals were kept, which included horses, mules, cows, goats, hogs and pigs.

There was a large barn where the special animals were kept and fed. The milk cows were kept in a separate area at night. We got our milk from them in the morning. If the cow was in a bad mood, she would wait until you had the bucket almost full, then she would kick it over and run away. That depended on who was milking her. I learned that even cows have "picks". The calves were kept in a special area until it was time for them to be with the cow for nursing.

There was a large area of woods where all sorts of trees grew ("the woods") where all the families cut wood for the fireplaces in their homes. There was a large area where we planted cotton ("the cotton field"). The fields were plowed in the spring of the year, and the cotton seeds were planted. The crops were worked in the summer, and harvested in the fall. The cotton was taken to an industry ("a cotton gin") where it was separated from the seeds and shipped to a cotton factory where it was sold, and woven into materials for clothing, linens and many other uses. The seeds were used to make cotton seed oil, and some seeds was preserved to plant crops for the next year. There was another area where corn was planted, "the corn field." Corn was worked and harvested same as the cotton and was used for cooking for family meals.

When it was dried and hardened, the corn was then gathered and taken to the corn mill and ground into meal. The cobs were ground to make feed for hogs. The shucks were used for many things. There was an area where melons, sweet potatoes, peanuts, peas, cantaloupes and sugar cane grew. Everything was worked and gathered by hand.

When I was old enough to go to the field with my parents, I began to notice the handy work of a mighty God! I could see the grass, the trees, the sky, the sun, the moon, the stars; I began to touch, feel, and smell things that I had never touched before. I experimented with breaking leaves from trees, flowers (wild) ones, pulling up grass, observing roots, smelling and tasting them, catching bugs, butterflies, worms, frogs, playing with baby chicks, baby puppies, baby pigs, but never baby kittens.

Church as a Child

When I was nine years old, I remember going to Sunday school with my father, and paying attention to what was being said, the singing, teaching, and when we stayed for church, the preaching and the people shouting. My sister, Cora Lee, and I would come home and pretend that we were the people at church. We would act out their performance; it was very exciting to us.

I was a very big girl at the age of nine when I heard talk about salvation, about heaven, and hell. I believed what they said and I began to think about how to make choices for myself. I knew I didn't want to go to hell, I wanted to learn how to go to heaven. After continuing in Sunday school, I was able to understand much more and at the age of nine, I accepted Jesus Christ as my Savior and made a confession before the church. After that I began to pay more attention, and sought to learn more about life for myself, and chose to do the right things and to obey, which brought the fear of the Lord into my heart. The best way I knew that I could please

God was to please my parents and do all that I could to make them proud of me and God would surely bless me. Exodus 20:12 "Honor thy father and thy mother, that thy days may be long upon the land which the Lord thy God giveth thee."

My father was a deacon and Sunday school teacher at the church we attended every Sunday (Hunters Chapel Missionary Baptist Church). He also taught us about the Bible every day. I don't remember one night that I saw my father go to bed before reading his Bible. Sometimes he read by the kerosene lamp and sometimes by the light from the fire place. We only had two bedrooms with two beds in each room. We only went to our bedroom when it was time to go to sleep. Our parents' bedroom was also the family living room. There was a fire place that burned wood and we all sat around the fire with our parents when our daily activities were completed. We also studied our school assignments by the fire light many times.

Home

S ometimes our bedroom wasn't very warm. Our mother would heat the clothes pressing iron, wrap it with a heavy bath towel and put it at the foot of our bed to keep our feet warm at night. If it was very cold, she would get up through the night and reheat the iron and put it back in our bed. Our father would put big logs of wood in the fire place before going to bed at night to make sure the room would be warm when we got up the next morning to get dressed for school.

Our mother would wash some of the smaller children's clothes at night by hand and spread them on the back of the chairs to dry after we had gone to bed so they would have clean clothes for the next day.

When we came home from school every day, each one had chores to do, sometimes the older siblings would rotate their chores. When the boys were old enough, our father would take them to the pasture to drive the cows to the cow lot to be milked and to also nurture their baby calves. Others would gather up small branches of wood to kindle the fire for the next morning. Others would feed hogs and pigs, while the older sisters would feed the chickens and gather eggs from the hen house for breakfast the next morning. There were plenty of chores for everyone. Our mother would prepare supper and take care of the baby.

When it was dark, we would come inside and have supper, then we would gather around the fire place. Some would sit in the chairs, some on a small bench or on the floor. Our father sat at the end of the circle, and taught us Scriptures from the Bible and also about the way of living in the world. He taught us how to work for a living with our own hands and not depend on anyone else as long as we could work for ourselves.

Mother taught us mostly about how to take care of our bodies and how to do things the right way, like how to cook a decent meal, and how to properly make a bed. She also taught us how to make sure the dishes were washed and put away correctly, to wash our clothes and how to hang them the right way, and how to love and care for one another. If we didn't do what we were told to do the right way, she would make us do it over again. She also taught us to get on our knees and pray every night before we went to bed.

Although mother and father have gone on to be with the Lord, their teaching is still alive in our hearts. The first prayer we learned to pray was:

"Now I lay me down to sleep
I pray to the Lord my soul He'll keep
If I should die before I wake
I pray to the Lord my soul He'll take."

We repeated that prayer every night before we went to bed. We did not understand what it meant, but when we said it, we went to bed with confidence, and went to sleep without fear. Although we heard people talking about how witches, and haunts, and devils, roamed around homes, and streets at night, we believed that God heard our little prayers. We also heard that the angels watched over little ones and we believed that our parents too were watching over us while we slept.

Although young, we had our own secret prayers that we never shared with anyone, for even at a very young age we knew that our parents did not know exactly how we thought and felt but we believed that we could tell God, and *He wouldn't tell anyone.* When we got older, we would share some of our secrets through personal conversations.

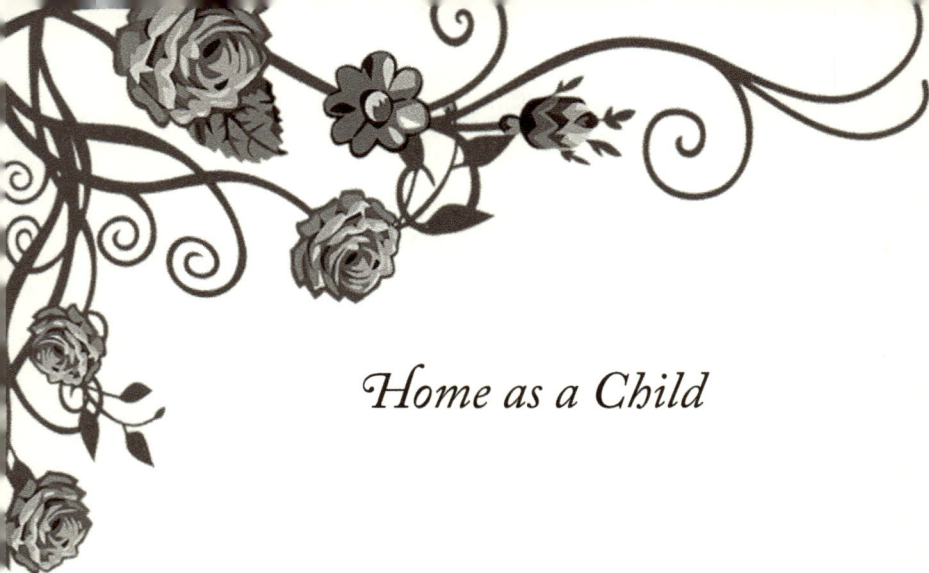

Home as a Child

We never went anywhere alone. Our mother would always see to it that wherever we went, it would be two of us; even when we went to the public restroom. Whether it was two big sisters or one big sister and one little sister, one always stood outside of the door and waited for the other.

There were three pairs of us girls and one odd that was our youngest sister, so she just fit in wherever she desired. The older sisters always watched over our little brothers. The younger brother, Leroy, was always quiet, but the older brother, Robert Earl, was very mischievous. My parents would leave him in my charge when they were not present and that was a tough job.

We lived in the country and there was no running water. We had to carry water from the well in buckets (water buckets). We had a large barrel that we would fill up for house use that would last at least two days, but for drinking water, we had to pack fresh water from the well at least twice a day.

We didn't have a refrigerator, we only had an ice box (a large wooden and metal box that looked like a small chest with a door that opened). We didn't have a hand sink, a facial sink or a bathtub; we had what we called a <u>wash pan</u>, that we used to wash our hands, face, and head, and a <u>small tub</u> to wash our feet, and sponge bath, and a <u>large tub</u> for taking a bath, and washing our clothes. (A no. 3 size tub that held about ten gallons of water), but even so, everything was done in order.

We were taught respect and love for one another, and even today, it is very hard for me to function in an unorganized group. Parents are their children's first teacher. It is much easier to train than to untrain, that's why Proverbs 22:6 says "Train up a child in the way he should go and when he is old he will not depart from it." Also "firm footing is guaranteed in shaky times." Proverbs 3:25-26.

We all ate at the same time with our parents at the table that our father built. Our mother always portioned out the food; she fixed everyone's plate to make sure that everyone got the same amount of food except our father, he always got a double portion. As we grew older, we understood why.

We were happy at home with our parents and our sisters and brothers. We didn't know anything about hate, or hurting anyone. If one was sick or sad, we all were sad, we did all we could to comfort one another.

I remember when my second sister under me, Margaret, was playing with some of the others; she was running and fell on the stump of a tree that had been cut with an axe and left a sharp point. She fell on it and split her knee. Mother didn't want to look at it; I didn't want to either. We couldn't get to a doctor; we lived five miles from town, with no transportation and our father was not around. I became her hero, without even knowing anything about first aid. I know the Holy Spirit showed me what to do. I had seen my parents put kerosene on bruises and sprains. I got a pan of water, washed it then applied kerosene to the wound. I then cut two strips of my mother's white sheet and pulled the cut area together and wrapped it over and below the cut. My sister never went to the doctor for the injury but it healed and she still has the scar. Jesus is still healing today if we will believe. One thing I do believe is that children eating the right kinds of foods will cure some conditions the same as medicine, but only Jesus can heal.

We didn't have a telephone. When someone got sick and needed a doctor, someone would go and get a horse and ride on the horse to the doctor's house. You didn't even know whether he was home or not, because there was no phone to call; you had to just hope that he was. You had to go around to the back door and carefully ring the bell or knock, and talk to him through the door.

The doctor would get in his car and go to the patient's house, then the person would try to make it back on the horse as fast as he could. All riding horses had to have horseshoes put on their feet, because they had to run on rocky roads and hard pavement. Horses were the only transportation most Black people had at that time.

The only way people could get messages to one another was by standing outside of the house calling as loud as they could, whistling or waving a cloth or a hat, but glory be to God, the messages got where they needed to be most of the time. The other way was by mail, but the mailboxes were a mile away from most people homes, at least for those who lived in the country.

The word "I love you" was not expressed in my childhood days. We only expressed love by showing it, or by writing it in a letter. I never heard my parents say to each other, "I love you". They never called each other any other name besides their own. In those days, that was a private word used for certain persons. My parents never told me that they loved me. The only expressions I heard them say was "I love the Lord Jesus." Mostly when you heard that, it was in a song. Our parents showed love by how they took care of us; they encouraged us when we did something that they liked, they would smile, and say "That is very good!" and sometimes they would give us something special. Our father would bring us something when he went to town for which had not asked.

Parents never know how some of the things that they do and say impact the future lives of their children. When I was growing up, most children did not ask their parents questions about the things they said or did; they just tried to figure it out in their own mind, or discuss it among their other siblings or their close friends. Sometimes you got it right, and sometimes you got it wrong. Many people today try to justify their shortcomings because of what their father or mother did or did not do when they were a child.

I have heard so many people, even Christians, say they weren't going to make their children go to church because their parents made them go. I have heard parents asking their small children what food they like, when the child didn't even know that they had a choice. So the child would stand there not knowing what to choose, so they choose whatever they wanted even if it wasn't healthy. When it comes to getting up and being ready for school, the child has no choice. Also when lunch is provided for them at school, they have no choice. Oh, what mixed emotions some parents impose upon their little children without even realizing it.

When parents tell their children to pick their coats up off the floor, and put away their toys, I feel certain that they think it's not being disobedient to say, I don't want to. When we were old enough, we helped carry water from the well; we used a large bucket. We never said "I don't want to." When it rained, we would put buckets and tubs out to catch rain water, which was used for cooking, washing, bathing, and sometimes for drinking.

Our father built a little shed, that he called the smoke house, where he would store our meats when he killed hogs. We would watch him butcher the meat. After he cut certain parts, he would put the meat on a table, or a large board, and sprinkle and rub it with salt. After that, he would put it into a large wooden box that he made and sprinkle more salt. The ham and the shoulder he would wrap with what was called a gurney sack cloth, and hang it up on a rack (in the smoke house) until such time that the meat would be used for the breakfast entrée, especially when we had guests. Our mother would prepare diced fried ham, scrambled eggs, homemade buttermilk biscuits, and sorghum molasses. The side meat was used to make bacon. The liver, heart, intestines, feet and tail all were used. That was called poor folks kind of food. White people would give those parts to Black people with large families, who did not raise their own hogs. Today those parts are as expensive as ham and bacon. We had to remove the shell (shucks) from our corn and take it to the corn mill to be ground into meal so that we could make corn bread; we also had to cut and detassel the sorghum, and take it to the sorghum mill to make molasses.

We would use flour and fertilizer sacks to make window curtains, pillows, chair covers, bed sheets, and pillow cases. I made a work shirt for my father and a pair of rompers for my little brother, Robert Earl. (Rompers were coveralls with a flap opening behind for little boys.) My aunt taught me how to sew on her treadle sewing machine. The first dress I made was for my sister, Willie Lue, who was two years younger than me. When I really learned how to handle the sewing machine, I made an outfit for my mother. She was really proud of it. She even wore it to church. She told her friends that her little daughter made her outfit. They didn't want to believe her. After that experience, I developed a great urge to sew and I have been sewing ever since. My parents impacted my life greatly by encouraging me in the things that I took upon myself to learn. Intellectually, children need to learn by seeing, hearing, touching, smelling and tasting. Opportunities to explore and discover should be given. There should be faith in their ability to learn from both parents and school teachers. A child's first and continuing education begins at home. Educators believe that the first five years of a child's life are crucial to his or her development. It is believed that fifty percent of a child's character and personality is developed by the age of three; seventy-five percent by the age of five. This is why it is so important for mothers to be at home as much as possible during the early years.

There is one thing that our mother and father told us that wasn't true, and we were so disappointed when we found out that Santa Claus was not real. For Christmas, our mother always baked eight to ten cakes. We would hurry to get our little decorating done. Our mother told us that if we weren't in bed and asleep at a certain time, Santa wouldn't stop at our house and if he did stop, and found us awake that time of night, he would put ashes in our eyes. So we made sure we would go to bed and would surely be asleep. She told us that we could sample the cakes, especially the coconut and chocolate ones. The other untruth they told us was when a new baby was born. They told us that the doctor brought the baby in his medical bag, and when there was no doctor, they said the midwife brought the baby in her suitcase (luggage) and gave it to our mother.

There was a crossroad near our home. Rich White people would bring their children's broken toys out in the rural areas and dump them on the side of the road. The Black children, (and sometime there would be a few Whites), would go through the rubbish. They would find broken toys; there were some with one arm or no legs or a little car or truck with three wheels, sometimes there were old school books, and coloring books, sometimes there was a little wagon with only three wheels on it. Our father would make a wheel. The boys would have much fun playing with it and riding in that wagon.

When I see children in Africa and India today, it reminds me that we were only a step away from what they are doing now. The only difference was our parents raised and grew our food, we didn't have to dig in the dumps for it. As time passed on and crops got better, our father was able to buy all of us new toys. Sometimes it seemed that crops would not be successful due to the weather; sometimes there were problems with too much rain or a drought and also the little enemies, the boll weevil, the army worm, and the stinging worms which would come when the cotton was in full maturity and destroy the leaves and the cotton bows. I remember seeing my father walking across his field with his hand behind his back and his head bowed, he was praying to God about the conditions of his hard labor and how he would take care of the family if his crop was destroyed.

Our young people of today will never imagine the burdens, the worry and the struggles that their parents endured trying to provide for and take care of their children when they had to work in the fields in the hot sun five days a week. They often had to carry their little ones to the field, leaving them under a tree at the edge of the field, going back and forth watching them to keep insects from harming them. They couldn't leave them at home; sometimes other small children sat and watched their younger sister or brother. Most Black people lived on the White man's plantations and had to walk home from the field to prepare the meal for their family, they'd carry their babies in their arms, and return back to the field and chop cotton until the sun was almost down. Our family was blessed, not having to live on a White merchant's plantation.

I wonder if some children knew the burdens, and hardship, their parents suffered under slavery and plantation life and everyday life to provide for them, whether they would have the heart to be as rebellious and disrespectful as they are today. Many parents don't have to struggle like my generation, however some parents still walk away because they don't want to be bothered, and leave their little ones to be brought up by strangers, mostly because of their own choosing and being disobedient to the Word of God.

Chopping and Picking Cotton

We used a hoe with a six-inch-wide blade in the cotton field, or corn field, which was acres of land, the rows were about twenty-four inches apart. We did this from six o'clock in the morning until six o'clock in the evening, with about one hour to rest and eat lunch. Our mother would go home earlier to prepare supper for the family. After supper, our father would sit down and read the Holy Bible and tell us about the Word of God, then we would get on our knees and pray.

Picking cotton means putting a sack over your shoulder, dropping it along beside the cotton row, picking the cotton out of the bow, pulling it off the ball, one ball at a time and putting it into the sack, until you filled the sack. The sack was six to nine feet long and when you filled it up, you would put it over your shoulder and take it to the place where the cotton was to be weighed. Sometimes the men had seventy-five to ninety pounds of cotton in the sacks. Most of the time, the women used the eight feet sacks which would hold approximately fifty to sixty pounds.

The cotton was emptied on the ground until there was enough to fill up a big high framed wagon, which would be about fifteen hundred pounds, then the cotton would be taken to a cotton gin, where it was separated from the seeds. They would sell the seeds, and give the worker half of the money that was paid for the seeds, which was called <u>seed money</u> to feed their families, which was a very small amount. Then they had to wait until all of the cotton was gathered from the field, before they could receive any of the money received from the sale of the cotton.

Those who lived on White merchant's land had borrowed money from the land owner to get through the summer months until the crops were gathered. Even at that they never received a statement or receipt as to how much they owed. They just had to take the land owners word for how much they owed, whether it was right or wrong. There were some families that worked hard, the father, the mother, and all the children that were old enough, and when the crops were gathered, and the father went to the merchant's office for his settlement, some were told that they didn't have any money coming, that they barely made enough to repay their loan, and were sometimes even told that they didn't make enough to pay the entire debt. The father then had to go home, and tell his family "We didn't quite make it out of debt this time, maybe we will do better next year. I will try to borrow enough to make it through the winter with a few things for Christmas." I am sure that you could never believe this could be a true statement, and naturally you wouldn't. I am sure that you never heard of such.

My father taught me about plowing in the field with the mule. I learned how to put the bridle on his head and the bits in his mouth. I learned the mule's language. When you wanted him to turn right, you said "G" and when you wanted him to turn left, you said, "Ha" and when you wanted him to go straight you said "Get-E-Up."

The equipment used for plowing was:

- The turning plow
- The middle buster
- The side harrow
- Section harrow
- The cotton planter
- The six inch hoe
- The five inch hoe

The hoes were used mainly for chopping cotton, corn and other plants. There were others chores such as picking cotton, pulling cotton, pulling corn, detasseling corn, and picking and thrashing peas. Peas were thrashed by first putting the peas in a large cotton sack and beating them with a stick until the peas fall out of the hulls, then putting them into a large container and pouring them back and forward from one container in the open air until all the hulls would blew away with the wind. This was called "winnowing peas."

My father taught me how to help him cut wood for the fireplace. He taught me how to cut wood with the axe and also how to use the handsaw and the chain saw with him. I thought that was really extraordinary. I didn't think there was any better thing to do than pulling and pushing the chain saw back and forward to my father until the big log of wood fell apart!

My sister Cora Lee and I were the two oldest of the children, that's why they named me Owen after my father; the boys didn't come until later. My father had a shot gun he kept on the wall in a gun rack in his bedroom. I begged my father to let me shoot it, it was his hunting gun. He told me that I wasn't strong enough. I told him that I was, so he showed me how to hold it tight against my shoulder when pulling the trigger or it would kick me. I forgot to follow the instructions. I pulled the trigger and the gun kicked me backward and I fell on the ground. That was the end of my gun career.

The fireplace was used for many purposes: for heating the cloth pressing irons which were called "the smoothing iron" to heating the straightening comb we used to straighten our hair; for drying clothes, to heating water. There was a special bar installed across the fire place that our mother used to boil certain foods, such as greens and peas in a large, black cast iron pot.

During our relaxing time, when we would play games, our father would roast sweet potatoes, and peanuts in the fireplace. He would lay them on the bricks in front of the fire and cover them with the hot ashes until they were done. That was a special treat for us. Our parents reserved all of our resources and so did most families who lived in the country. They didn't throw away anything that was good and usable, when they peeled apples to can, or to make an apple pie, they would boil the peeling to make apple jelly. They made jelly from plums, and preserves from strawberries and pears. They even preserved watermelon rinds which were used to make rind pickles and the seeds were saved for planting the next year.

We made our own table syrup with White cane sugar, and our own pancake mix. We used White flour to make starch to starch our clothing, window curtains, men's blue jeans and also to paste wall paper on walls. We used grease from pork meat to make lye soap which we used to wash our clothing and for other household chores. We also used okra to water wave our hair, okra on wet hair and Vaseline makes beautiful hair waves.

We made sleeping mattresses with a strong fabric called orgam burg, a real thick and tough fabric, we filled it with hay from the hayfield. Our grandmother saved up enough feathers from chickens to make feather mattresses, and feather pillows. We also made sleeping mattresses with corn shucks. Think that's strange? These items were called hay ticks and feather ticks.

I always heard people say that, Our Lord and Savior was born in a manger, filled with hay. When I read the King James Bible it says that he was wrapped in swaddling clothes lying in a manger, because there was no room in the inn." (Luke 2:7) According to Webster, manger means a trough where horses were fed. Swaddling clothes mean: the long narrow bands of cloths wrapped around a new born baby in former times.

Today when babies are born, they are born in hospitals, in special wards and with the best of care. If the question was asked "Why was our Lord and Savior born in a manger when God owns the earth and all that dwells within it?" I believe the answer is because our father God so loved the world, you and me, that He gave his only begotten son to be born the lowest, and the poorest, so that if we would believe in Him, that we would become joint heirs with Him in the Kingdom of God.

I and most of my siblings were born on a bed with a <u>hay tick</u> mattress made by hand and filled with hay from the field, which was used for feeding farm horses and mules. When we saw our little baby sister or brother, we were as amazed as the shepherds when they saw Baby Jesus.

I remember when the Governor demanded that all people must purchase factory made mattresses for their families to sleep on. Where there were large families, some of their children slept on sheets, pillows and quilts. Most of them were made from sacks that the feed for animals came in; some from fifty-pound flour sacks. I suppose that was called the lowest, and the poorest, but can you believe that we were all happy? That was our life.

Our father was amazing. We always wondered how he knew about so many different things, we thought that he knew everything. The only book that we saw him read was the Holy Bible, it was a large Bible with the portrait of Jesus, and other Bible characters, and people of the Bible times.

He never allowed us to handle the Bible; of course we didn't, but we loved looking at the pictures, and trying to figure them out. The Bible was not a book that children played with. We learned to respect the Bible because it was the Word of God.

Our father told us about all the creation and how God made the earth, the seas, the moon, stars, sun and all the animals and man. I had never heard the song, "He walks with me and he talks with me, and tells me I am his own." It was many years later that I read and sang those words. The thoughts and feelings I had about what he taught us came rushing back to me. Even as I am writing now, those feelings and thoughts are so real. There was something within me that I could not explain. When I was a child, when I woke up in the morning, and looked out of the window, and saw the sun shine, and the dew on the grass sparkling like diamonds, and beautiful colorful butterflies, and the little birds singing, it was so wonderful to me. We didn't have song books in our home, not even sheet music, but there was a song in my heart, and a prayer on my mind. It was like I was singing, "Over my head I hear music in the air."

Early in the morning when we got up, we always heard birds chirping, often times we would ask our father what they were saying. Our father told us that they saying, "Get up, Get up! Laziness will kill you!" When we heard the owl hooting at night, we asked what they were saying; he told us a story about how the old owl was a very stubborn kind of bird who never learned to build a nest because when birds were given instruction as to how to build a nest, the leader would say, "Take one straw, and a little mud." The old owl would say, "take two, take two," so he got angry and flew away saying "take two take two." He never learned how to build a nest so he is still sleeping on a limb of a tree in the woods at night, hooting, "Take two, take two." So as I listened, that sounded just like what they were saying. Anyway, that answer was good enough for me because I believed that everything our father told us was true.

School as a Child

The school I attended was held in a church building. The name of the church was called "Hunters Chapel Baptist Church," that was the church of which we were members. I don't know whether the church was named after our grandfather, or named after my grandfather's slave master. We had school five days a week, Monday through Friday, then we had church there on Sundays. Sometimes church meetings and programs were held on Saturdays. Our home was about one mile from the church, and we walked there for school and church. Our father always took the wagon on Sundays for our mother, and the small children. There were other families who did the same. Only a few people owned automobiles in those days.

The church/school had a tall iron heater that sat in the middle of the floor. It was the parent's responsibility to provide wood or coal to keep the room warm for the children. Some parents were not able to do either. Those whose parents did not, or could not participate in the supplies, felt uncomfortable and would not strive for the comfortable seats. They would just kind of stand back and pretend that they were not cold. The children who knew that their parents were able to help provide took priority over the ones who could not. We took our lunch in a brown paper bag or sometimes there was a little jelly bucket with a handle and a lid. We called it our <u>lunch bucket</u>. Some had lunch boxes that they bought from the store; some didn't have any lunch at all, they just pretended they were not hungry. Sometimes we took jelly biscuits, molasses biscuits, egg or fried pork. We only had water to drink. In 1935 a school lunch program was provided for the children of poor families, especially in the rural schools, where mostly poor Blacks lived.

For school, we had only one book each, and some of the children did not have any. They would copy their school assignments from other children or the teacher's book. I remember the year when the government provided new books so that every child could have their own. They brought them to the school in a large wooden crate. That was a very joyful day. All the children went home with new books. The teacher, whose name was Ms. Cindy Davis, issued the books out to the children according to their grade. We had only one teacher. She taught from first through the ninth grade. While one class would be involved in class review, the other class would be studying. Sometimes the higher grade students would help teach the lower grades. There were no inside restrooms and no running water. Some children did not go during the whole day. Today children, and often times adults, cannot sit through a Sunday school class without going back and forth to the restrooms. I suppose having a nice place to go makes a difference.

I want you to know about the struggle that Black children had coming up in the south. Walking to school in the cold, rain, snow and heat, most of the time with only one pair of shoes, and sometimes one change of clothes. If it wasn't for the cooking lard, and meat grease from the bacon, there wouldn't have been oil for their hair, or skin.

School buses would pass by loaded with White children, and they would poke their heads out of the window and spit at us, and call us "nigger". In the summertime the roads were just plain dirt. When a car passed by, you would have to get as far on the side of the road as you possibly could and try to cover your head and face to keep from getting covered in red dirt or muddy water.

The other sad thing about school is if you couldn't get your assignment done, the teacher would whip you with a long switch, (a small limb from a willow tree). If the student was a big boy, the teacher would make him lay across a chair and two other big boys would hold him, while she gave him a number of licks. They used a ruler on the younger children for misbehaving.

I believe that action was a carryover from slavery. The people had a slave mentality. I know most people can't believe that this is true. This is not a Black history book. It's just the reality of what I have heard and seen growing up in the state of Mississippi.

After completing the last grade of elementary school, I attended Como High School for one semester, and became discouraged because I was living with my father's cousin. She was an elderly lady. My father rented a room in her home and paid her for my meals as well, which I shared with another girl who was in the same grade.

Cousin Dolly was a widow and her son lived with her. He was a school teacher and was very nice, but his mother, Cousin Dolly was a very mean, harsh lady. The room that we slept in was very cold. It was a very cold winter. Cousin Dolly would order coal for the heater which she used to keep the home warm. She would have the delivery man to dump the coal on the ground, outside of the shed and have us pick the coal up with our hands one piece at a time and put it into the shed so that the coal would not break or crumble. I was stressed out and afraid living there, but I knew how much my father wanted me to get a high school education and to go on to college and become a school teacher. He really felt that I had the full potential of becoming a school teacher. I had to figure out a way to get out of school because I knew that living with Cousin Dolly there was no way that I could keep up with assignments and learn when all I could think about was how I was being treated. I was trembling inside with anxiety most of the time.

Unsung Heroes

There were so many unsung heroes that never got honored right there among us that no one even recognized because they never knew that common people could be heroes. And if they did, there was no means of publicizing it.

There was a Black man in our community who dug wells without any training or any special tools, using a hand shovel. The well had to be sixty feet deep. There was a group of men who built a wooden scaffold on which he sat. It must have been made of gofer wood. They would let him down into the well with a rope and when he needed to come out, they would draw him back up. They continued this process until he struck water. No one seemed to think about any danger that could happen. I wasn't old enough to know just all that happened, but I do know that when it was finished they attached a (whirl reel) with a rope through it and a bucket on each end, and we had good cold water for drinking and all of our other water needs. He never made the newspaper and no one seemed to think that much about it. But later in life I realized that he was our hero, and God gave him the knowledge to make it possible for us to have good water.

The Lord our God in Heaven has brought us through so many dangers, toils and snares and kept us safe. So many times we lived through danger, and didn't even realize it. We can truly say as David in the twenty third Psalm, "though we walked through the valley in the shadow of death, so many times walking through high weeds, dark wooded area, where there were all kinds of animals, snakes of all sorts, barbed wire, sometimes encountering wasps and stinging bees, honey bees, and bumble bees. And so many other strange species that could have harmed us… But it was only God who kept us safe.

I remember when my grandfather died, I cannot remember the date. I was only about ten years old. I remember he was in a hospital, in Oxford, Mississippi. He called all of his children and grandchildren that were old enough around his bedside. He talked to all of them before he died, about what he wanted them to do about the home, the land, and Grandma Luevenia.

I remember he beckoned for me to come closer to his bed. He had a terrible hiccup and the nurse kept giving him sips of water. I remember he told them to bring him a spool of white thread and they brought it to him. He told them to take one strand and break it in half and they did. Then He told them to break off three strands and put the three strands together, and they did. Then he told them to break the three stands; they could not break them by hand. The lesson was to demonstrate how hard it would be for the family to be broken if they would just stick together; as we grew older, our father taught us that same lesson.

I heard adult people say that after a family member dies that they come back. I would go to the side of the house and walk toward the well where my grandfather would go and draw water, and then go to the pond and water his horse before they went to the field. I thought I would see him, but it didn't happen. So I finally gave up but I never told anyone. That was my childhood secret. Sometimes adults are talking around children and think they aren't listening but most of the time they are.

Unfortunately, we never had a picture of our grandfather nor any pictures of his parents. We never heard our father say anything about his father's parents, so we didn't ask about them. We were just children and it didn't even occur to us. We were happy that Grandpa Allen was our grandpa because he always gave us what we asked him for, mostly clothes, candy, quarters and dimes.

Our grandmother, Luevenia was a great cook. She always had some foods or cookies for us. We were told that her family was from North Carolina. They were separated during the slave trade and she never knew what became of her parents or other family except one sister who she found later in life. Our grandfather found a few cousins but none of them ever mentioned anything about their parents. They were Christians but I don't know how they learned about church; the only Church we knew about was the one we attended as children. Our grandmother told us about the prayer meeting that they would have at their home. When they met to pray, they would turn a wash pot upside down in the middle of the floor to keep the sound from being heard by their slave masters.

I was about thirteen years old when our home burned to the ground. It was a very sad day. Everything we had went up in flames. Our mother and father made sure that they got all the children out, but were not able to get anything else out. Our mother and father was standing away from the blaze and smoke with all the children standing with them. Our mother was holding the baby, our little brother in her arms. Different neighbors came and invited us to their homes. We were separated until our father could get another house built. I went to the home of one of my best friends who I went to school and church with. Her parents were very nice to me, but I had never stayed away from my parents and siblings before. I tried to act happy but I cried every night when I went to bed. Our father finally got another house built. Later our Uncle "Nelse" moved to Memphis, Tennessee and gave his two room house to our father. Dad had the house pulled and attached it to our new house. It was a different style and size and it made the house look different but it provided us enough room to be more comfortable.

When my older sister, Cora Lee, was seventeen years old, she went to Memphis, got a job, and stayed with our uncle and aunt. Her job was at the Baptist Hospital. When I was 14 years old, my parents allowed me to go there too. When school was over for the summer, I also got hired at the same hospital in the special diet kitchen. I worked until school started back in the fall.

Home as a Teenager

Our father had taken us to Memphis a few times to shop for clothes and to visit his sister (Aunt Mary) and it was so much fun. I didn't have to worry about getting lost because I was with my family, but when I went to stay for a while and had to travel on my own, it was not the same. My sister showed me where to get on and off the bus. After I had done it several times, I felt very comfortable going by myself. I didn't know that there a certain area for Blacks and one for Whites only. One evening I got on the bus, coming home and sat in the Whites only area. I was instructed to the area that was for Blacks, and it was jammed and packed. There were only enough seats for about eight people, others had to stand up.

There was a Black divider between the area where the Blacks sit and a small opening enough so you could see the street where you got off. There were vacant seats in the White area, and there was a Black man who got on the bus later. He just sat in one of the vacant seats. There was a White man sitting in the seat behind him and he asked the Black man to get up and go to the Black area. The White man said, "No nigger is going to sit in front of me". The Black man replied, "I paid my fare the same as you." The next thing I saw was the two hitting each other.

I had never seen anything like that before. I didn't know anyone on the bus. I was the only teenager on the bus. I didn't have a phone; I didn't even know anybody's phone number. The first thing I thought was that I would never get home and see my mother and father and sisters and brothers again. I thought that was the last of me. The police were called and the men were taken off the bus. I think every woman on that bus had some kind of weapon in their purse. They started hiding them under the seats of the bus when the police were called. My uncle was upset when I got home. He was waiting for me with his belt because he thought I was just being disobedient.

He didn't wait to find out why I was late. When he found out what happened, he was sorrowful but I was so hurt, I had already had the worst scare of my life and now he was waiting for me with a belt. There were no apologies and even if he did, I wouldn't have known how to accept it. After that, I was ready to go home because I could never believe that he had any confidence in me. As much as I loved my uncle, I never felt the same about him again. That was my first bad experience out in the world. I told my parents about what happened on the bus but I never told them how my uncle treated me.

That was an experience that I had to live down on my own, through my prayers to God. Even at fourteen, I learned how to put my faith in God. I had been very sheltered growing up. That was the beginning of the hard experiences in the world. Now I can attest to the fact that an false accusation when you cannot defend yourself is next to murder, not unto death, however. But it can surely kill the feeling of a good spirit that you have toward someone. Even at a young age, the old granddaddy of liars, the devil, wants to kill and tarnish the reputation of God's people. When deception and delusions become overpowering, we are to stand fast and hold the traditions which we have been taught whether by words or by our epistle (II Thessalonians 2:15).

After the summer school break was over, I came home after working my first public job, making only $9.50 a week. When I got paid, it was not by check. They just handed cash to you in an envelope with the amount written on it. No taxes were taken out. I had earned $47.50 a month. That was more cash than I had ever had in my hands. I wanted to go and buy something for my parents and all my siblings. I came home, sweet home. Then it was time to go back to school. I learned so much from working and doing things that I had never done or seen before. Preparing and taking food trays to sick rooms, prepared me for mission work. The values, and essentials of serving, and foods itself, never left my mind. I desired to learn more about it.

I came home and my sister continued to work as an assistant baker. She later got married and shortly after she got married, she became ill and never regained her health.

She remained ill until she died. There again was another devastating experience in my life. We were the two oldest children in the family. She died at the age of twenty-one. She wanted to come home so her husband brought her home. And she didn't live very long after that; she died at home. That was a horrible experience for all of us. No one knew that she was gravely ill until it was too late. I was at a loss. She was my best friend. We mostly did everything together. We slept together; we went places together. We would talk ourselves to sleep at night. I was then the odd one. I didn't know how to pray about death; I felt helpless and depressed and lonely.

When the hearse came to take her away, all of us children just clung to each other. Our mother went to the other room; she didn't want us to see her emotions. Our father just stood in the yard and watched as far as he could. We didn't know what to say to each other. It was really a blessing when our friends and neighbors came to comfort us. Most parents find it difficult to talk to their children about death. But death is just as real as life, just as we prepare our children to live, they must be prepared to die. When children are old enough to understand, we must begin to teach them about death, keeping in mind that all children do not comprehend at the same pace or level.

I would suggest the following to start with:
- Teach them love;
- Teach them to share;

- Teach them to smile;
- Teach them to obey;
- Teach them to respect others;
- Teach them about God, our heavenly father;
- Teach them about salvation (Rom 10:9; 6:23);
- Teach them the Lord's Prayer and explain it to them.

Home as an Adult

The greatest hurt I ever experienced was when my mother died. I was on my way to visit my family on a Saturday with my two sons, Rufus and Robert. I decided to stop in town first. Just as we entered the street, someone met me and told me that my mother had fallen dead. I do not know who it was that told me, but I just started saying, "no, no." I was so shocked, I lost my feeling and began feeling numb. Momentarily, it seemed that the whole world changed.

I felt that I had lost my best friend and my last friend, as if my heart would shut down. My husband rushed me to the house only to find my mother lying on the floor and all my sisters and brothers standing around her crying. My father went to get a doctor but it was too late. I remember my auntie picking me up off the floor; by that time, I stood up. I saw a long Black hearse in our yard. That was the second time a hearse had come to our house. Our mother didn't have a chance to be helped. No one even knew that she was that sick. She just fell to her death. She was braiding my little sister's hair. Our mother had a four-month old baby, our little baby brother. Our knee baby sister, Kenyaka, was about three years old.

My two sisters who were the oldest at home had to become sister/mother for the household. Our little brother, Moses, died about three months after our mother died. The youngest sister didn't remember our mother long. When someone asked about her mother, she would say "Willie Lou and Margaret". They were her sisters, but she began to think they were her mother. They were both just teenagers, but they stood in the gap. Two years later, our father remarried; he married a lady named Lena Jennings."

I was very disturbed when I heard that my father was going to get married. Not because he was getting married, but I didn't know how a stepmother would work out with someone who had seven children at home and she would bring two of her own. Although I knew that our father was a praying man.

It was amazing how it all worked out and we were all able to get along. My oldest brother was twelve years old and the next week, after our mother died, he started washing his own clothing. Every time I went home and saw Robert Earl trying to do things that he had never done before and didn't really know how. It really broke my heart all over again.

Our parents never talked to us about what to do in a death situation. Most of our conversation was about life. We knew school mates who had lost their parents. We tried to sympathize with them but we didn't really know how it felt until we lost our mother. We often heard people singing a song about motherless children having a hard time when mother is gone. It was a sorrowful song. Just hearing that song, made me feel sorry, even before experiencing it, but today I can attest to the song: "I know the Lord will make a way, Yes He will," "God will bring things out alright." "He never left me alone". (Scripture: They that wait upon the Lord shall renew their strength; they shall mount with wings as eagles; they shall run and not be weary; they shall walk and not faint." (Isaiah 40:31). "Wait on the Lord; be of good courage and he shall strengthen thine heart; wait I say on the Lord" (Psalm 27:14).

Home as Children

Even though as a child in the state of Mississippi, we were happy together in our neighborhood; These are things that we did for fun:

- Bouncing balls
- Sally go around the sun shine
- Tug of war
- Rolling old car tires down the road
- Tom walkers
- Jack rocks
- Rolling wagon wheels
- Playing checkers
- Used car tires for swings (tied on a limb or tree with a rope)
- Making mud cakes
- Rag balls (we made ourselves)
- Rubber soft balls (store bought)
- Bail hay wire, nailed on the outside of the house with two bricks between each end on the wall, played as a guitar

- Used large limbs from a tree for baseball bats
- Bucket lids nailed on a plank of wood rolled it down the road called it scooter
- Sling shot: made with rubber from a tire inner tube tied it on a stick from a tree
- Cost My Handkerchief Yesterday
- Shoo Fly, Don't Bother Me
- Tap dancing
- See saw

These things kept us busy. We felt free, happy and safe.

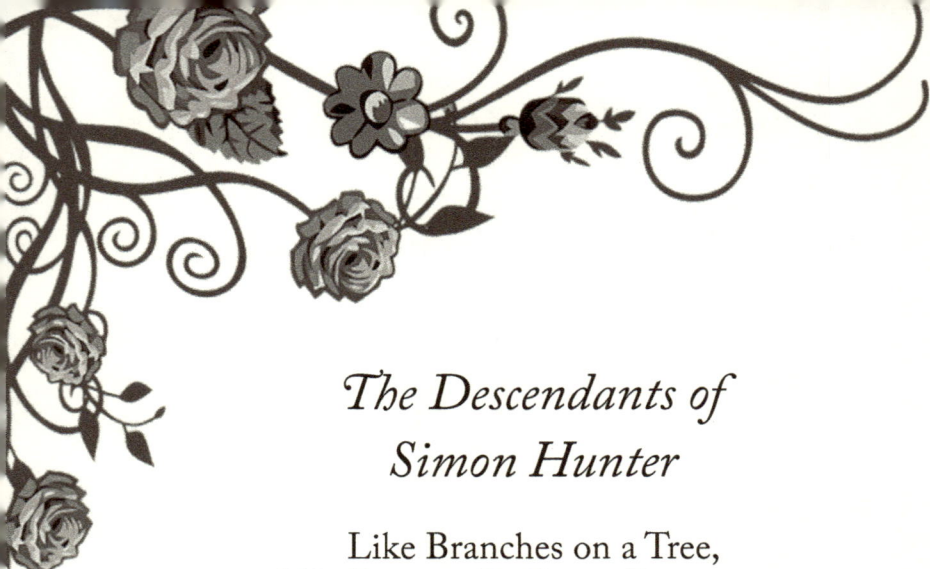

The Descendants of
Simon Hunter

Like Branches on a Tree,
We Grow in Different Directions
Yet Our Roots Remain as One

My family has spread out across the United States as far away from Mississippi as California, Georgia, Illinois, Louisiana, and Tennessee. And yet we see the impact our parents had on our lives still resonating in us today. Our parents always told us that we could be anything we wanted to be. And we believed them. Most of us have accomplished far more than we dreamed as children growing up in Mississippi. I have already outlined my accomplishments, and this is just a bit of information about my siblings and their accomplishments:

Cora Lee Hunter was my oldest sister and my best friend. Her death at the age of 21 left a void in my life that has never been filled. But my memories of her are very precious. At the age of 17 she became a Desert Baker for a hospital.

Willie Lue Hunter was my next sister. She passed away in 2015. Her first job in Danville was a hotel maid. However, she only kept that job a short time. She acquired a job with the Veterans Administration, where she retired with excellent benefits and enjoyed taking it easy and living a life of retirement for more than 20 years. She was also a Quilt Maker and a Florist and member of a gospel singing group for many years.

Margaret Hoskins is my next sister. She also worked as a hotel maid when she arrived in Danville. She later went back to school and earned her Associates of Arts degree and worked as a certified teacher's aide. When that program was abolished by the government, she opened her own business and began making wedding flowers and gowns. She also sang in the gospel singing group and organized many Church programs. Even in her eighties, she is still hosting women's conventions. She is also a musician and an author.

Robert Earl Hunter is my oldest brother. He went from the cotton field and wagon wheels to the air plane and flying with wheels. From walking five miles to a small town to work to riding in his ocean air plane and flying across the country. He and his younger brother Leroy were very fascinated with airplanes. They would take cardboard boxes, cut them in pieces, and construct them as an airplane and tie a string to it and fling it in the air to make it fly.

When Robert Earl was nineteen years old, he enlisted in the Navy. When he came out of the navy, he went to Los Angeles, California, where he started a trucking business and later purchased his own air plane. After acquiring his pilot license, he flew across the country. He stored his airplane at the Danville Vermilion Airport. He took me for my first airplane ride. I thought we would never stop going up but when we started coming down I was holding my heart in my hand! He took everyone that would ride with him for a ride in the sky. He flew his plane to his hometown in Mississippi. He was the only Black man that I knew in Mississippi that owned and flew an airplane.

Leroy Hunter is my youngest brother. He left home at the age of 18, went to California, got married and was employed by General Motors. When he retired from GM, he moved to Haughton, LA. There he started his own business as a tailor and seamstress, went from blue jeans to tailoring trousers, for men and women, then to t-shirts with transfers and embroidery to wind breaker jackets and capes. Now he does t-shirts for family reunions, churches, schools, jackets and capes for companies. This is a God-given gift. He never went to a sewing class or learned by watching someone else. Now he hires his own help.

Clara King is my next sister. She is the oldest of the three younger sisters. They were the first that had the opportunity to finish high school and go on to college. After college, she worked as a social worker, and later for the Internal Revenue service. She had always wanted to be a criminal defense attorney like Perry Mason. At the age of 51, she decided to go to law school and earned her Juris Doctorate. She practiced law for more than 15 years and is now president and founder of Watchdogs for Justice, a non-profit organization formed to help keep kids out of prison. She is also a Motivational Speaker, Mission Worker, and Author and Book Publisher.

Rosie Milligan is my next sister. She acquired her RN license and worked at several hospitals. She worked as Director of Nursing for Job Corp before leaving to launch her own publishing company and returned to school to earn her Ph.D. in Business Administration. She has hosted "Black Writers on Tour" Conferences for more than 20 years which draws writers from all over the nation. She is also a motivational speaker, Talk Show Host, Author and Book Publisher.

Kenyaka Beckley is our baby sister. She finished college and went to work as a salesperson for Pacific Bell Telephone Company. She quickly became the number one salesperson in southern California. After she retired from her job she started her own business hosting family and community conferences empowering families for success. She also formed The Council of Elders, a non-profit organization that serves as a bridge between the community and local government agencies. Thank God for so many of our offsprings who have acclaimed careers such as: Doctor, Lawyer, Authors, Teachers, Nurses, Builders, Owners and Operators of Eighteen Wheelers, Mechanics, Preachers, Missionary Workers, Missionary Leaders, Social Workers, Managers, Police Officers, Beauticians and Business Owners.

We pressed forward because our parents told us that we could do or be anything we wanted to do or be, and we believed them. Maybe you have never had anyone to encourage you in that way. I want to let you know that your Heavenly Father is saying those very words to you today.

He says in Revelation 22:17, "Whosoever will, let him come and take of the water of life freely." Will you believe Him and go out and do and become whatever you have a desire to do or become? You just need to decide what you want to do and take the first step. He is waiting to help you.

God is no respecter of persons. He has given gifts to everyone but some have buried theirs and some have ignored theirs because they don't recognize them as a gifts from God. Obedience and faithfulness are the keys that unlock the door that will open ways for you that you could never discover on your own.

School

Iwas afraid that if I really told my father how my cousin treated me, he would not have believed me. We were always taught that we had to obey older people because they were supposed to care for you, and see that you did what was right. So I thought the only way that I could get out of this was to get married.

I didn't know anything about marriage; I only knew what I saw between my mother and father and that some of my school mates that had gotten married. I had not read anything about it. It was not taught in school. My mother and father had never talked to me about it. My father's dream was that I would go to college and become a school teacher. That was also my inspiration, but I knew that I could not study for test and meet the requirements of keeping up my assignments under that kind of stress and fear I was in while living with my cousin. I wasn't used to being around mean people, so I started thinking of how I could escape this embarrassing experience without disobeying or disappointing my parents.

When my boyfriend proposed to me, I had no idea about what his plans were, other than me being his wife. We didn't have any discussion or make any plans for marriage. The plans I had in my heart about marriage did not include him. The one I thought I would marry had been drafted in the army. When he came home on a furlough, he was going to be a father, so that was the end of that expectation. My next thought was, I knew my husband's family; they were good people; and he was so respectful toward me; I was sure the marriage would work out. And so we got married. He talked to my parents and they were surprised. They didn't know what had happened so they gave in to it. In those days, you just didn't get married without your parent's consent. The husband to be had to go to the girl's father and get his approval unless they decided to elope (run away) and get married.

I got married at my parent's home. It was not an elaborate wedding, just a few friends, neighbors and family. That turned out to be an awful experience. I didn't know anything about sex. There again, I tried to figure out a way of escape. I cried all night. I felt as though I was incarcerated between the devil and the deep blue sea. Only God could take care of young people in such situations. That's why it is so important that parents bring their children up in the fear and admonition of God because He is our Creator and he knows more about us than parents can ever know.

After three months, when I found out that I was going to be a mother, I realized that I had stepped into a whole different world. I was no more daddy's little girl. Now I was going to be responsible for someone's life. In those days, there were no sonograms, not for Black women anyway. My husband (Phillip Bobo) found a house for us to live in on a White man's plantation. I had never lived on a White man's plantation before, which was another terrible experience for me. Leaving my parents' house was a very difficult thing for me. It was very sad leaving my younger siblings.

The day when I was leaving, we were moving in a wagon with a very small number of things to move, such as a bed, dresser, chair, and a table and our clothes. When we had gotten about a mile away from the house, driving down a long graveled, dusty road, I looked back and saw my little brother, Leroy, running trying to catch up with me. My husband stopped and pulled the wagon to the side of the road, and waited for him. My mother didn't know that he had left the house. We had to turn around and take him back home. He was determined that his oldest sister was not going to leave him behind. He was very exhausted when he got to us.

My husband and I became share croppers on the plantation. That meant the plantation owner had a contract with you in which he would give you a certain amount of money at the beginning of each month until time to gather the crop. At the end of the harvest season, he would subtract the amount you owed from the amount you made from the crop. If your crop was successful, you could pay your debts, and have money to do the things that you needed to do for your home and family, but if it was not a successful year, then you were still in debt and had to work hard another year hoping that the next year would be better, again that was another horrible experience.

My husband was a very hard worker. One day he was plowing in the field it was so hot that both he and the mule were wet with sweat. When the owner saw his mule wet with sweat, he became so angry. After an exchange of words, he cursed my husband and struck him on the head. My husband came home with his nose bleeding and went to his friend's house to borrow a gun. But his friend wouldn't let him have it. There again, I didn't know what to do but one thing I do know is that God's grace and mercy was with me because I didn't want to tell my father, and surely wasn't going to tell anyone else. I only trusted God with all my heart. I was so afraid I didn't know if it was over or not.

So we moved from that plantation to another. I never knew that anything like this could happen; it was like a nightmare to me. I was a long distance from my parents. We didn't have a car and I didn't have anyone to help me with my baby son and on that plantation I had to take my baby to the cotton field with me. My husband was born with the gift of carpentry. He built a little playpen and took it to the field for the baby to stay in under a shade tree and covered it with a thin net cover. I made a little mattress pad and a pillow for him. I had to chop cotton and walk back and forth all day to nurture him, and keep him dry and safe from the insects.

I know this seems unreal to the younger generation, but every bit of this is true and more. There were many young mothers and husbands who experienced the very same thing.

They did whatever it took to take care of their little ones. There was no such thing as a child care center for Black people and it didn't matter whether a woman had one child or ten. They had to work in the field and all of the children that were old enough had to work too. If some young people knew what their parents went through, would their attitude toward their parent be different?

After three years, my husband didn't want to live on a White man's plantation any longer and neither did I. Because of all the stress, anxiety, and disappointment, he decided to go to Memphis, Tennessee and got a job and a place for us to live. I moved back home with my parents. My husband went to Memphis and found a job. My oldest child was two years old and I was pregnant with the second one. I had been through so many devastating experiences I was afraid to move to a city not knowing what the living situation would be. My second son, Robert, was born at my parent's home. When my baby was old enough, I went with my husband but I couldn't see taking my little ones to live in that environment so that was the end of our marriage.

When my oldest son was five years old, I remarried. My two sisters, Willie Lue and Margaret asked me to give the two boys to them; the youngest was three years old. I told them that I would give Rufus to Willie and Robert to Margaret. They were so happy. They told our father that I was going to give the boys to them. He just laughed and said, "Don't you know that she didn't mean that."

Sometimes people are overwhelmed by the number of problems they have, the duration and the complexity of the problems. When people have been depleted of their strength they need outside help. When I was a young woman, you couldn't go to an older person and tell them your marital problems and you couldn't talk to anyone in your church either. Most people would tell you that what goes on in your home or family should stay in the home.

Everything that was written in the past was written to teach us, so that through endurance and the encouragement of the Scriptures, we might have hope (Romans 15:4). Whenever there is a marital problem or family problem, we should always talk to God first. Ask for guidance and help. Above all else, we must ask for the power and ability to conduct ourselves as Christians as we attempt to deal with our problems and issues.

I write these things, some of what I have experienced and some of what I have seen. America is a world leader among affluent nations, yet it is full of hurting families. We are constantly reminded by talk shows and behavioral scientist of the overwhelming numbers of dysfunctional families. According to statistics between 40 and 50 percent of all marriages in America will end in divorce. We all see the result of those broken homes in the broken and bruised lives of families, especially children, torn apart by divorce.

There are many road blocks to identifying problems in marriages. You cannot solve problems that you cannot identify, especially when we do not practice the presence of Christ in our families. I believe the most common road block to solving our problems is not having the fruit of the Spirit, which is: Love, Joy, Peace, Patience, Kindness, Goodness, Faithfulness, Gentleness and Self-control.

Some of the biggest fights in marriage can be over a woman who does not know how to cook, and a man who cannot fix anything. Considerations that need to be met in someone else's life should be clearly understood before marriage.

Move to Danville, Illinois

My husband, Tom Nelson, and I moved to Danville, Illinois, on the first day of January, 1956. It was the coldest day I ever remembered. His cousin, E. L. Nelson, came to Como, Mississippi, in his big truck and moved us to Danville. I had never been to Danville before. We left my two sons with my family until we found a house to rent. When we found a house they were put on the train by themselves in care of the train conductor. Rufus was eleven years old and Robert was nine. They had never ridden on a train before. We met them at the train station. I had never been away from my sons that long. I was so glad to see them.

We enrolled them in school right away. It was an elementary school about four blocks from where we lived, and they were two happy boys. We started looking for a jobs. We had been told that you could always get a job here in Danville, but that wasn't a true statement. The first job we found was at the Wolford Hotel and to our surprise I got a job as a maid cleaning guest rooms. My husband was hired in the housekeeping department. My wages were 44 cents an hour and his was 54 cents. We were so disappointed. We brought money with us but it didn't last very long. We had never had to pay house rent, water bills and telephone bills before so the money we had didn't last very long. In Mississippi, we raised most of our foods and vegetables, but we had to buy everything in Danville. Oh how I wish that I had stayed in Mississippi. The owners at the Wolford Hotel treated the employees as if they were slaves. I was so surprised. They treated us a lot worse than the Whites in Mississippi had treated us.

We didn't bring our car with us to Danville. We sold it when we moved from Mississippi; therefore, we had to ride the bus to work. It wasn't very long before I got a job at the Lakeview Hospital, working with special diets. I had previous experience in food service on my first job in Memphis, TN at the Baptist Hospital. My wages at Wolford Hotel in 1956 was about the same as I made in 1942 in Memphis when I was 14 years old.

My husband finally got hired at General Motors. My two sons, Rufus and Robert, started working when they were twelve years old at Mr. Shields Shoe Shine. They started working without pay. The customers would just give them tips and when they turned thirteen, Mr. Shield started paying them fifteen dollars a week. They started out working for free, just to learn how to work on a job. They have been workaholics ever since. Even now you will not see them just sitting around doing nothing. When they were old enough, they went to work at General Motors and when they got married, they both bought their own homes. That was just a part of their heritage because almost all of the Hunter families were hard workers and owned their own homes.

Church in Danville

The first church I attended when I moved to Danville, Illinois, was the Richard Temple COGIC. I met Pastor Richard's wife working at the Wolford Hotel. We became friends and she invited me and my sisters to their church services. I had not attended any other church in Danville because I had to work on Sundays and they held their services at night. So my sisters and I began attending their services on Wednesday and Sunday nights.

They never had an altar call or never opened the doors of the church. There were no offerings taken; the service was simply singing, testifying, praying and reading Scriptures. It was really different. We grew up in a Baptist church which was very organized. Richard Temple was a Church that came together on one accord to praise and worship the Lord and tarry for the presence of the Holy Ghost. I will never forget that night; the gentleman was playing the piano and singing "There Is Something Within Me." That was the first time that I got out of myself and really let myself go. It seemed that I was caught up and started moving toward the front of the church as if I was on wheels. Before I got all the way to the front, it seemed as if something took hold of me and just softly laid me on the floor as if I was a baby. As I lay there, I began to speak in a language which I did not understand. I tried to refrain, but I had no control. When we left Richard Temple that night, I began to feel and think differently about many things and I had a better understanding of the Bible.

That church did not last long under the city's inspection, and shortly afterwards Lauhoff & Company purchased all of the property on that street. When I was given Sundays off, I started attending Mt. Zion Baptist Church which was the closest church to where I lived. There were times when we had discussions about living holy, the Holy Ghost and speaking in tongues. I know that the baptism in the Holy Spirit and speaking with other tongues is real, because I experienced it myself. But I never believed in arguing about religion or the scripture. In the second epistle of Timothy, Paul writes, "Study to show yourself approved unto God, a workman that needeth not be ashamed, rightly dividing the word of truth." (2 Timothy 2:15). "But ye shall receive power after that the Holy Ghost is come upon you." (Acts 1:8) "And they were all filled with the Holy Ghost, and began to speak with other tongues, as the spirit gave them utterance." (Acts 2:4) My two sons also attended Richard Temple. It was amazing and fun to them. After Richard Temple, they attended Snday school at a Baptist Church near our home.

From my youth, I was inspired to teach as my father had wanted me to be a school teacher. My greatest inspiration was to teach the Word of God. After I started studying and searching the word, the greatest problem I encountered was that I never found many adults who wanted to really take the time to study the Bible.

I united with and served in three churches in Danville. I loved my pastors and all the members. They were all great preachers and teachers. I always tried to do my best but I never reached my desired goal, my greatest satisfaction occurs only when I believe within myself that I have done my best. When we moved from that side of town of the city to where we live now, we purchased our home and united with the church which was in walking distance of our home; Mt. Zion Missionary Baptist Church where the Rev. Simeon Edwards was pastoring. We were able to see our children and their children grow up in Mt. Zion church. My first assignment was to sing in the senior choir. The next was to teach the Youth Sunday School class. I was able to teach my grandchildren as well. I was later assigned as the missionary teacher, which lead to a deeper study and understanding of the Bible.

I later united with Antioch Missionary Baptist Church where I was appointed Christian Education teacher and leader, Missionary teacher and appointed to the Courtesy Committee service under the leadership of Pastor Lucius Barber. I also sang in the senior choir.

I was a working mother and wife all at the same time. I never stopped serving in the house of God and made it my priority. When I was not able to perform my assignment physically, I learned to comfort and encourage myself in the Lord by quoting the Scripture, "Man looks on the outward appearance, but God looks on the heart".

I thank God that every job that I started where I was scheduled to work on Sundays, it wasn't long before my supervisor made arrangements for me to have Sundays off. It seemed as if they were seeing through my heart, as if it was a heart to heart situation.

I also served in a newly formed local church, the Freedom Missionary Baptist Church which was started under my cousin, H. L. Reed. That was the first church that I had helped to organize. I organized the choir and mother's board and also taught the Adult Sunday School Class. Rev. Reed retired after two years of pastoring there; he turned the church over to a younger pastor, Rev. Jerry Wilson. With the permission of my Pastor at Antioch, I served at Freedom for two more years.

It was really edifying to work with the young people, who were so eager to learn the Word of God. After they were well on their way, I went back to my home church where I united with the church mothers and missionaries. I attended Midwest Baptist College in Danville to further my knowledge in Church mission work. The class was very inspiring, but I also had the experience described in Ecclesiastes 12:12 which says, "And further, by these, my son, be admonished: of making many books *there is* no end; and much study *is* a weariness of the flesh."

I found out that many people aren't interested in learning any more than they already know after they reach a certain age, because they never do the things that they have already learned, especially from the Bible. Some believe that it is impossible to learn more. So that was a lesson that I had to learn, it was just like having your wardrobe filled with too many clothes; you can't wear but one outfit at a time and one pair of shoes. I found out that learning can be weariness as well; we are forever learning and forever experiencing things in this life.

Church in
Mississippi-Revivals

Most of the pastors in Churches in Mississippi lived in the city or towns that were from fifty to a hundred miles from the church they pastored. During the weeks of revival, the church members took turns keeping the pastors in their homes. The first seats across the church were called the mourners bench, where all who were seeking salvation would sit whether they were children or adults, but mostly children from the ages of nine to thirteen. The church mothers and deacons would counsel; the mothers would counsel the girls and the deacons would counsel the boys. The saints would meet every day at the church for prayer. The service would start at seven o'clock in the evening. The seekers were told to separate themselves from their playmates who were not seeking salvation during the week of revival and to refrain from eating too much heavy food, but just focus and pray and rest.

During the church meetings you could hear the people singing from a long distance away because there were no air conditioners or fans in the church so they had to leave the windows open. Some brought hand fans from home; some used cardboard, some fanned with their handkerchief; even so there was so much love and fellowship during those meetings. The preacher would stay outside under the shade tree because he did not have an office. The deacons would start devotion singing hymns and praying. The choir did not sing in the choir stand during revivals; everybody sang congregational songs.

After the revival was over, the converts were baptized. The baptism was held at the closest pool to the church, which was in an open pasture where the animals came to drink water, which was a very large and deep body of water. The deacons would measure the depth of the water, according to the height of those who were to be baptized. The preacher did not go in the water alone. There were always two deacons who went in with him and helped with the burying (or dipping) of the converts and bringing them up from the water. It was a beautiful and sacred occasion as the families waiting on the banks of the pool sang "Take Me to the Water." The mothers were waiting with white sheets and towels as they brought them out of the water. There was no dressing room. They just took them to the wooded area behind the church to change into their church clothes, but everybody was happy. Although we have modern things today, I still appreciate the experience of how God was in the midst of His people in those days. We appreciate modernization, that our Lord Jesus has allowed us to see, but yet, "eyes have not seen, ears have not heard neither has it entered into the hearts of man the good things that the Lord has in store for those who love Him."

Danville Community

In the year of 1958, I joined an organization in my neighborhood called the Elmwood Community Playground and Civic Group. The group was implemented by two special men in the community, Rev. Otis Wheeler, who was a minister, and Amos Williams who was a deacon of the church in the neighborhood. They saw children growing up in the neighborhood who had no recreational outlet. There was no park nearby for the small children to play. Their parents did not own an automobile to take them to the city park, which was too far for them to walk. They could play in the street or in their yard. None of the houses had large yards. The houses were very close to each other and the street was muddy. One day my two boys were comparing where they lived in Mississippi to the streets in Illinois. They decided that they would rather walk in the red dirt in Mississippi than to walk in the black mud in Illinois.

The organization was wonderful and helpful to the whole neighborhood. They sought many ways and means to help all the children and adults in the community. All the people in the neighborhood joined in. The organization was instrumental in acquiring a park and a building with equipment for learning and constructive activities for all the children in the community. The children went on field trips and traveled to places that they had never been. Most of the young people who grew up in this neighborhood have moved away. Some got married; some went away to college and chose to live elsewhere. There are only two older persons in this area now that were originally a part of the community's organization at the beginning.

Rev. Otis Wheeler and Deacon Amos Williams implemented a grass roots program, and they organized it and made sure that it was built on a Christian foundation. They were men who looked out for all the children and especially the teenage boys by searching the city and all the industries. They also looked at every work place that was available to find jobs for those that were old enough to work after school.

There was no standing around on the streets at night. Every boy in the neighborhood had a job doing something. Those who didn't have a job were in some type of sport, such as basketball or football. The girls that were old enough were participating in school activities, some helping at the Laura Lee Fellowship House; learning fitness awareness; participating in special achievement programs; and some singing in the choir. Their involvement and the interest of the leaders had a great impact on their lives, their development of character and enhanced confidence in themselves.

My granddaughter, Tina Nelson was a very adventurous child; she started reading the newspapers at the age of five. She was very observant of her surroundings and became involved in social agencies and activities as a teenager. She started a six-week summer camp for children in the community park which was held every summer for ages 5 to 15 which has continued over the years. There was also a 4-H group and a Cherish the Children Group held on Saturday mornings in the building. After the departure of Rev. Otis Wheeler, the remaining members: Deacon Amos Williams, Mrs. Clara B. Davis and Owen L. Nelson were instrumental in re-organizing the Charter and launching the program to a greater dimension.

Aging in Danville

Aging in Danville is far from what I saw among our families when I was younger. Among our family we cherished our elders and it was always a privilege and an honor to be around them just to sit down and talk with them. We cherished and had great respect for the older generation in our midst. Whenever you came into their presence, they were always departing wisdom and knowledge which was very inspiring to us. Most every home had an elderly person and there wasn't any such thing as a nursing or assisted living home. Older people who owned their home, always had some among their family to come and live with them when they were no longer able to maintain their home by themselves. Older people never stopped going to church, unless they were physically unable to go. The Church always honored their presence and faithfulness, their hard work was never forgotten. In these days, older people are forced off the public job, whether they are still able to work or not; some are being ostracized in the church and many are left lonely at home.

Too many are forced into nursing homes and left in the hands of strangers, where they will never feel comfortable, useful, or even loved again.

Many younger people don't appear to care to even be in the presence of older people, unless there is some great benefit for them. Some will never know or consider the inconvenience and suffering that some parents endured just for their well-being. I remember my grandparents, their life and their death. My parents did not live to be as old as their parents did; my mother died at the age of forty-four. My father lived to be eighty-two and I took him into my home. He lived with me and my husband until he became ill enough to go in the hospital. He was sent to a nursing facility for a very short time when his condition was beyond our ability to handle, but he was only there for a very short time before he died. He didn't linger in his suffering but I took care of him for eight years in my home. The very sad thing that I see in the present time is that there is very little respect given to the older people and very little care in the homes, in the streets, in the church, or in other places where the elderly happen to be.

No matter where we are, and what condition we are in, there is one promise that we can always count on. And that's the promises of God Almighty who gave His Son Jesus Christ who died for us all, that He will never leave us alone, as long as we trust in Him.

My husband died when I was fifty-five years old. My grandson, Robert Jr., stayed with me until he was old enough to go to high school, then he went back home to be with his parents and sisters.

I took foster children into my home. I attended foster parent training and became a foster parent. During my time as a foster parent, I had a total of fourteen children in my home. The last one who lived with me was a sixteen-year-old girl who had a nine-month old son. She lived with me until the baby was two years old, then she moved to another city to continue her education, after which I was alone again. I became very attached to them, especially to the baby. They became a part of our family and when they moved away, it was as another family member leaving home, but I continued being involved with my grandchildren and children in the community.

I didn't think about aging; I was too busy to think about myself until I experienced an illness. I had never taken prescription medicine on a regular basis before. Most of the time, when I went to doctors they described my illness with my age, as if I was feeling the way old folks should feel. But I didn't know because I had never been this old.

I started thinking about my age when my grandchildren started getting married, having their own children, and moving away to other cities. It was very different from when my own children got married, but I realized it was because they never moved far away from home. I thank God that they didn't, because they have been my only support since my husband died. I haven't had to worry about the maintenance of my home because my oldest son, Rufus, takes care of that; and when my car needs maintenance; I can always call my youngest son, Robert.

When my siblings started moving to other cities, it didn't seem so bad at first, because they all would come back to visit often, or I could go and visit them, and I was still busy with my church activities, community, and work. I didn't really feel the effects of growing old. Often times somebody will remind me that it is time to sit and rest, because you have done enough. Some constantly reminded me of how old I am as if I don't know how old I am, but it is my constant prayer to number my days and apply my heart to wisdom. One Scripture I keep in my heart is that the "seed of the righteous will not be forsaken and his seed will not have to beg bread." (Psalm 37-25) I have no regrets in getting old; what saddens me the most is the separation from relatives and friends, who have departed this life, and those who are not in the ark of safety. The only safe place in the world today is in our Lord and Savior Jesus Christ.

Get Wisdom, Get Understading

While I was writing, I stopped for a moment and picked up my Holy Bible and when I opened it, it opened to the first chapter of Proverbs, the proverbs of Solomon:

"To know wisdom and instruction: to perceive the words of understanding" (Proverbs 1:2)

"A wise man will hear and will increase learning and a man of understanding shall attain unto wise counsels" (Proverbs 1:5)

"Fear of the Lord is the beginning of knowledge; but fools despise wisdom and instruction." (Provers 1:7)

Wisdom is life and health:
"My son, attend to my words; incline thine ear unto my sayings. Let them not depart from thine eyes; keep them in the midst of thine heart." (Proverbs 4:20-21)

When I was young and watching the elderly women in my community and in the church, I imagined getting older would be a wonderful, peaceful, restful, and time of contentment in my life. It seemed that old folks had nothing to worry about; they were done raising their children, and didn't have to go out and work anymore. They all had rocking chairs and early in the morning when they got up and started their day; they could sit in their favorite chair and someone would bring them their coffee and breakfast platter. When they went to church, they were loved and treated special by the church members. They didn't have to worry about how they were going to get anywhere because their children or neighbors always looked out for them. When they would sing Dr. Watt's songs and hymn, it would edify the church. Today, there are still elders who could be going to church, but don't have anyone to help them get there and don't feel a part of the family anymore; they cannot sing the contemporary songs and be comfortable with the loud and speedy music. Otherwise, those who are able to go on their own are tied down with their great and great-great grandchildren. I don't have grandchildren around anymore. It really takes some getting used to being alone day after day, especially when you grew up in a large family. I spend more time reading the Bible which brings great comfort when I am all alone. I really feel the void in my life by not being able to do so many things that I have been used to doing for so many years. I sometimes feel useless to just sit and not be able to do things in church, go to the nursing homes to sing and comb people's hair, and sew and bake. I miss being able to get in my car and drive myself to the doctor's office and any other place I needed to go. I thank God for home health care and Faith-In-Action, which has helped me so much. Most of the people seem to be as old as I am, but they are still out there helping other old people. (It is God's amazing grace!)

The Need of
Salvation in the Family

A world trying to make it on their own.
Parents trying to make it on their own.

Children trying to make it on their own.

Churches trying to make it on their own. They are just spinning their wheels in the mud of futility because without God we cannot do anything good and purposeful. So many people feel that being three times seven is all that it takes to be able to do as they please, but please believe me that no man is an island. You cannot get through this world by just being grown. You are surely going to need someone's help and you definitely need God. What if your parents had not kept and fed and taken care of you when you were a baby and what if the church didn't have members? How would there be a body? How would the doctor's practice if there weren't any patients? Everybody and every institution needs someone in order to be complete and fulfill its function. The President of the United States needs a cabinet and the voices of the people. Everybody needs somebody. Every male needs a female, every man needs a wife, and every woman needs a husband. Each and every body needs God who is our Creator and Savior. Today we are living in a time of spiritual warfare. I have shared much about my life, and what I have experienced. I am sure some of what I have shared is amazing, some surprising, and some unimaginable, but I don't want to close this writing without including the Word of God. I hope that you can gain something from it that will inspire you to search the Scriptures and find it in the Bible for yourself. If you are helped by what I have shared, and pass it on to someone else, it will become a chain reaction for many and also an inward awakening to an authoritative approach to spiritual warfare. We have all heard that the devil comes to kill, steal and destroy! We as a people are in need of spiritual awakenings. Some of the works of the devil are: sin, sickness, fear, death, depression, murder, temptation, deception, lust and rebellion. But I John 3:8 inform us, "for this purpose the Son of God was manifested that he might destroy the works of the devil."

Some have falsely attributed acts to God that were really of the devil. Ephesians 4:27 says "leave no room or foothold for the devil, give no opportunity to him." As Christians we must put on the whole armor, the shield of faith, helmet of salvation, belt girted with the truth, sword of the spirit, breastplate of righteousness, feet shod with the preparation of the gospel.

Hosea, the prophet, warned the Hebrews, "My people are destroyed for the lack of knowledge." "Faith cometh by hearing and hearing by the Word of God" (Romans 10:17). The word is our cornerstone of faith.

We do not believe that Christians can be demon possessed. But they certainly can be attacked in their mind, will, emotions, and body. They can be troubled, pressed, buffeted, harassed, depressed, obsessed, in bondage and bruised. These things can hinder their relationship with God. They may still hang on to a form of godliness but it is only an empty shell camouflaging their spiritual condition.

Matthew 6:24 and Luke 16:13 "No man can serve two masters, for either he will hate the one and love the other, or else he will hold to the one and despise the other. He cannot serve God and mammon."

James 3:11, 12 "Doth a fountain send forth at the same place sweet water and bitter? Can the fig tree, my brethren, bear olive berries or a vine, figs? So can no fountain both yield salt water and fresh?"

I Corinthians 10:21 "Ye cannot drink the cup of the Lord and the cup of devils; ye cannot be partakers of the Lord's Table and of the table of devils."

I Corinthians 3:16-17 "Know ye not that ye are the temple of God, and that the Spirit of God dwelleth in you? If any man defile the temple of God, him shall God destroy; for the temple of God is holy, which temple ye are."

Can you imagine demons running in God's holy temple?

I Corinthians 6:19, Know ye not that your body is the temple of the Holy Ghost which is in you, which ye have of God and ye are not your own?"

I John 4:4 "Ye are of God, little children, and have overcome them: because greater is he (God) that is in you than he (devil) that is in the world."

I Corinthians 2:12 "Now we have received, not the spirit of the world, but the spirit which is of God; that we might know the things that are freely given to us of God."

I John 5:18 "We know that whosoever is born of God sinneth not; but he that is begotten of God keepeth himself, and that wicked one toucheth him not."

Remember "...though we walk in the flesh, we do not war after the flesh; (for the weapons of our warfare are not carnal, but mighty through God to the pulling down of strongholds;) casting down imaginations, and every high thing that exalteth itself against the knowledge of God, and bringing into captivity every thought to the obedience of Christ." (II Corinthians 10:3-5)

"Submit yourselves therefore to God. Resist the devil and he will flee from you." (James 4:7)

The Spiritual Challenges That We Face Today in the World

It is not God's will for His children to live in constant bondage. John 3:36 says "If the Son shall make you free, ye shall be free indeed."

"Be sober and vigilant; because your adversary the devil, as a roaring lion, walketh about seeking whom he may devour; whom resist steadfast in the faith, knowing that the same afflictions are accomplished in your brethren that are in the world." I Peter 5:8-9

In our world today, as we watch the news on television, and listen to the radio and just listen to people converse, we constantly hear about tragedies, hatred, killings, and controversy. So much so until even Christians fail to mention the Word of God after we finish those conversations. The next day we repeat it over and over; we forget about listening to our gospel music that we love to listen to, so therefore, we live in an environment that takes our mind and our heart completely away from what God would have us to do.

The people that are holding our attention are faithful daily in what they are interested in and what they have hope in. It seems that God's people have put their duties on hold, until this or that is over, but few ever return to press for the prize.

They know that when this plan subsides, the devil has another plan waiting to take its place. He has some scheme to entertain until you have completely gotten away from the path of the Lord hoping that you can go back and pick up where you left off later. If you continue on that path, the Word and your intent to get back to God's will and plan for your life will be completed removed from your heart, then you will have to try starting all over again, but it may be too late. (Food for thought).

Spirit of Divination

ACTS 16:16-18
- Fortune teller; soothsayer - Micah 5:12; Isaiah 2:6
- Warlock, witch, sorcerer—Exodus 22:18
- Rebellion—I Samuel 15:23
- Stargazer, Zodiac, Horoscopes—Isaiah 47:13, Leviticus 19:26, Jeremiah 10:2
- Hypnotist, Enchanter—Deuteronomy 18:11; Isaiah 19:3
- Drugs (GK Pharmakos)—Galatians 5:20; Revelation 9:21; 18:23; 21:8; 22:15
- Water witching/divination—Hosea 4:12
- Magic—Exodus 7:11; 8:7; 9:11
- Roots.. works of the flesh—Galatians 5:19-21
- "By their fruit ye shall know them"—Matthew 7:20

Matthew 18:18
Bind: the Spirit of Divination
Loose: the Holy Spirit and Gifts—I Corinthians 12:9-12

Why God Hates Divination

Divination leads people to seek satanic intelligence for guidance in their lives instead of God and His word, we cannot mix the guidance of the Holy Spirit with that of Satan without getting into problems. Millions of people in our world are doing just that when they consult their horoscopes instead of God's word for their daily direction.

Cartoons and Toys

Parents should be aware of the occult teaching that is being written into cartoons for younger children; they are being programmed with Eastern Mysticism and witchcraft practices. Take time to find out which ones are taboo for your child.

Familiar Spirits

LEVITICUS 19:31

- Necromancer—Deuteronomy 18:11; I Chronicles 10:13
- Medium—I Samuel 28
- Peeping and muttering—Isaiah 8:19; 29:4; 59:3
- Yoga—Jeremiah 29:8
- Clairvoyant—I Samuel 28:7-8
- Spiritualist—I Samuel 28
- Drugs (GK Pharmakos)—Galatians 5:20; Revelation 9:21; 18:23; 21:8; 22:15
- Passive Mind Dreamers—Jeremiah 23:16; 25:32; 27:9-10
- False prophecy—Isaiah 8:19; 29:4

Seek God's Guidance

God's method of directing the lives of His children is found in His divinely inspired word. The psalmist tells us God's word is "A lamp unto our feet, and a light unto my path." Psalm 119:105

"But the Comforter, which is the Holy Ghost, whom the father will send in my name, he shall teach you all things and bring all things to your remembrance, whatsoever I have said unto you." John 14:26

"For God is not the author of confusion, but of peace, as in all churches of the saints."

I Corinthians 14:33

If we are truly walking with God, we also will manifest a humble and teachable Spirit.

Spirit of Jealousy

Numbers 5:14

Murder—Genesis 4:8

Revenge; spite—Proverbs 6:34; 14; 16:17

Jealousy—Numbers 5:14-30

Hatred—Genesis 37:3-8; I Thessalonians 4:8

Cruelty—Song of Solomon 8:6; Proverbs 27:4

Strife—Proverbs 10:12

Extreme competition—Genesis 4:4-5

Contention—Proverbs 14:30

Cause Divisions—Galatians 5:19

Envy—Proverbs 14:36

Roots "Work of the flesh"—Galatians 5:19-21

"By their fruits ye shall know them"—Matthew 7:20

According to Matthew 18:18—Bind: spirit of jealousy; Loose: Love of God

I Corinthians 13; Ephesians 5:2

Numbers 5:14—Isaiah 14:12-14; Ezekiel 2819; Matthew 12:36; Philippians 4:8; II Peter 2:1-2

Spirit of Heaviness

Isaiah 61:3

- Excessive mourning—Isaiah 61:3; Luke 4:18
- Sorrow; grief—Nehemiah 2:2; Proverbs 15:13
- Self-pity—Psalm 69:26
- Insomnia—Nehemiah 2:2
- Broken-heartedness—Proverbs 69:20; 15:3-13; 18:14; Luke 4:18
- Despair, dejection, hopelessness—II Corinthians 1:8-9
- Suicidal thoughts—Mark 9
- Depression—Isaiah 61:13
- Inner hurts, torn spirit—Luke 4:18; Proverbs 18:14; 26:22
- Heaviness—Isaiah 61:3
- Roots of the flesh—Galatians 5:19-21
- God has promised to be with us, working everything out for our good (Romans 8:28)
- "When thou past through the waters, I will be with thee and through the rivers, they shall not overflow thee" Isaiah 43:2

(The garment of praise is the most effective deterrent against the spirit of heaviness. Praise the Lord and Pray.)

The Spirit of Whoredom

Hosea 5:4

- Unfaithfulness/adultery—Ezekiel 16:15-28; Proverbs 5:1-14; Galatians 5:19
- Spirit, soul or body prostitution—Ezekiel 16:15-28; Proverbs 5:1-14; Deuteronomy 23:17-18
- Chronic dissatisfaction—Ezekiel 16:28
- Love of money—Proverbs 15:27; I Timothy 6:7-14
- Fornication—Hosea 4:13-19
- Idolatry—Judges 2:17; Ezekiel 16: Leviticus 17:7
- Excessive appetite—I Corinthians 6:13-16
- Worldliness—James 4:4; I John 2:15-17; I Corinthians 6:13-15; 18:20; I Timothy 6:7-12

"Therefore, brethren, we are debtors, not to the flesh to live after the flesh, for if we live after the flesh ye shall die; but if ye through the spirit do mortify the deeds of the body, ye shall live. For as many as are led by the Spirit of God, they are the sons of God." Romans 8:12-14

The Need to Evangelize Families–
What I Have Read and Experienced

A s I stated earlier, there were no marriage counselors in the area of the country where I was raised. If there were, our fore parents were not aware of them, and there was no literature available on the subject. Most marriages were absolutely done by trial, but with the prayers and the help of God, they stayed together until death. Today there is information and instructions about marriage and family commitment everywhere: schools, churches, newspapers, television, group studies, workshops, and above all the Holy Bible. In today's world, we see many broken homes, dysfunctional families, divorces and millions of children in foster care. Some of the children have to be placed in institutions, because there are not enough foster homes available.

There is a dire urgency for training married couples, and also single parents, about their commitment to their marriages, and child raising. There are some very important commitments that married people must make and these must become personal convictions. Christian couples must be committed to:

- God's will for marriage and family;
- The permanency of marriage;
- Loving each other with Godly love;
- Forgiving each other.

For too long, some of us have assumed that just because two people are Christians, they automatically have a Christian marriage. Married couples must be trained in the biblical principles of marriage and family. There are no perfect people so there are no perfect marriages. Therefore, there will be problems in marriages and families. We must preach, teach, train, and counsel families on how to live by Biblical principles.

God instituted marriage and family. Lawlessness, ungodliness and rebellion should not define Christian families. The Holy Bible tells us that God instituted marriage and family, not man. Man instituted divorce and living together in an uncommitted relationship. It takes three things to complete a marriage: a husband, a wife and God.

- God's purpose for marriage is for love and companionship (Gen 2:18; Malachi 2:14);
- God's goal in marriage is intimacy and oneness. (Gen 2:24);
- Marriage is a lifelong covenant with God that should be broken only by death. (Rom 7:2);

- Marriage should reflect the relationship of Christ and the Church (Ephesians 5:25, 32);
- Christ is the way to a successful family (John 14:6);

God's love is agape, or unconditional; it is not an on-again, off-again commitment.

Parents are Children's First Teachers—What I Have Seen

It is important that the extended family become involved in the lives of single and married parents. Sometimes the church serves as the extended family. Children need their parents, extended family, and the Church to play an active role in teaching and guiding them in the way they should go. When this is done, we can rely on the promise in Scripture: "When they are old, they will not depart from it". Youth ministries can help by initiating program activities to meet the needs of young people and help keep them on the right track. We all agree that it takes a village to raise a child. Homes, churches, schools and communities need to be vigilant and involved in helping to save our children.

Parents certainly need to be alert for adult drug users who may be in our families and may be careless in their irresponsible state. Often times, I see mothers smoking cigarettes while holding their little baby in their arms and feeding their little ones on the run. We often see little children with a bag of potato chips, cookies, or candy. I feel so sorry for those little helpless children who seem to be hungry at all times, whether in church, the store, or riding in a car. They always seem to be eating or drinking, and it's mostly junk food.

When I was a child, we had meal time with the family sitting at the table together. This is not the case today. Most of the time family members are eating on a paper plate or out of a paper bag. There is no need for spoons or forks anymore. When I was growing up we felt bad because there were not enough spoons and forks to go around. Some had to wait for one child to finish before they could have their spoon or fork. Is this what we call modern day advancement and intelligence?

Notes: Dr. Willie Richardson

Early education in child training and discipline should begin in the home. Two of the greatest problems in the home are lack of direction for children and the inconsistency of parents as to what they want and expect from their children. There should be home standards and rules that will please God, such as:

- No smoking allowed;
- No guest allowed in bedrooms; and
- Parents must know where their children are at all times.

Code of Conduct

- Willful disobedience. Result: use the rod;
- Willful disrespect. Result: use the rod;
- Stealing. Result: use the rod;
- Not cleaning room. Result: clean basement or some other room;
- Not washing dishes properly. Result: must be done over again.

"Do not withhold discipline from a child, if you punish him with the rod, he will not die. Punish him with the rod and save his soul from death." (Proverbs 23:13-14)

"Folly is bound up in the heart of a child, but the rod of discipline will drive it far from him." (Proverbs 22:15)

Please know that children are a gift from God trusted in your care to love and keep safe.

IF...

"If a child lives with criticism, he learns to condemn.

If a child lives with hostility, he learns to fight.

If a child lives with fear, he learns to be apprehensive.

If a child lives with pity, he learns to feel sorry for himself.

If a child lives with jealousy, he learns to feel guilty.

If a child lives with encouragement, he learns to be confident.

If a child lives with tolerance, he learns to be patient.

If a child lives with praise, he learns to be appreciative.

If a child lives with approval, he learns to like himself.

If a child lives with recognition, he learns to have a goal.

If a child lives with fairness, he learns what justice is.

If a child lives with honesty, he learns what truth is.

If a child lives with security, he learns to have faith in himself and in those about him.

If a child lives with friendliness, he learns that this is a good place in which to live."

--- The Watchman Examiner

Premarital Counseling Training

It should be understood that choosing the right spouse will determine the success of your marriage and that premarital counseling is only an aid not a guarantee of success. What couples need to understand is that the success of their marriage depends on the spouse they choose, not the counseling itself. Counseling will help them only if they have made a good choice in a marriage partner.

- There are many road blocks to identifying problems in marriage:
- Lack of empathy
- Inability to work through problems
- Lack of emotional stability
- Inability to give and receive love
- Self-centeredness
- Having bad attitudes
- Being selfish
- Poor communication skills
- Lack of motivation

- Relational problems
- Sexual problems
- Financial problems
- Spiritual problems
- Children problems
- In-law problems
- Past or present relationships problems

Couples must seek God's wisdom in working through these problems in order to achieve peace, security and reconciliations.

Premarital Problems

Husband - common and everyday problems:
- Sarcasm every now and then
- Stubborn behavior
- Drives without insurance and loans out car
- Usually interested in sex at inappropriate times
- Tells lies
- Wears dirty clothes
- Have clothes all over the house.
- Dirty socks under the bed and counter in restroom and middle of the floor anywhere he takes them off.
- Does not bathe regularly or keep hair clean and combed.
- Does not brush teeth often.
- Does not eat with family regularly.
- Last out of bed but will not make it.
- Does not put things back after using them.

Wife:
- Sometimes uses profanity
- Depressed often
- Difficulty in showing affection
- Harden because of long term rejection
- Feels bad about having to be the responsible leader, financially, physically and emotionally because he left it up to her.
- Have to say what's on her mind in front of the children, the only time available.
- Resents husband and regards him as a burden
- Lies often

These things may seem to be nothing to complain about but unconsciously eat away at your patience, heart, and soul and causes hurt and bitterness between couples.

I read about a church pastor who took a survey of the couples which he had married. The results were that 75 percent of the couples he had married had separated or divorced, 25 percent were still together, and only 10 percent of the couples were happily married. Of the 10 percent who were happily married, only half of these couples knew why they were happy. The Christian life is radically different from a life without Christ as Lord and Savior. We know that people who are truly converted, a radical change takes place in their lives, their morality and values change. In addition to their love of God, their love for self and for other people change. How they conduct themselves when dating also changes. When we make wedding vows, we are making a covenant with the person we marry and with God. You can't leave God out. He instituted marriage. Man instituted divorce and living together without commitment. "I hate divorce," says the Lord" (Malachi 2:16). Marriage is permanent until death. It is extremely important that parents teach their children about marriage vows and what's expected in a marriage and the importance of their commitment to one another and to God.

Parents should also teach their children about the sacrifices involved in family life; what to expect when the honeymoon is over, when responsibility sets in and when they become parents. Parents should be taught about the sharing of both parents and the patience and self-control needed in the caring and nurture of children. Parents should also let their children know that parenting is governed by God and under the authority of His word.

Parents should not discipline children when they are infuriated or when there is a question as to whether they are in control of their anger. Don't threaten or belittle your children by saying such things as, "you are just like your old daddy." 'I'm going to break your neck." "I'm going to knock your head off." "I'm going to bust your behind." "I'm going to skin you alive." Ephesians 6:4 says "Fathers, do not exasperate your children: instead, bring them up in the training and instruction of the Lord."

Many parents do not know that the words we speak are never forgotten and are stored up in the brain of the child and never forgotten. When they are old, the memory of those words still hurt. I know grown and elderly people who still shed tears about things their parents said or did to them when they were children. Those angry and bitter words still reside in their minds. We all need to remember that "children are the heritage of the Lord and the fruit of the womb is his reward." (Psalm 127).

We have heard and read about many historic men in the United States of America, and a very few women. Mostly those who we heard about were slaves. This listing of women was taken from a publication series "*An Empak "Historic Black Women*".

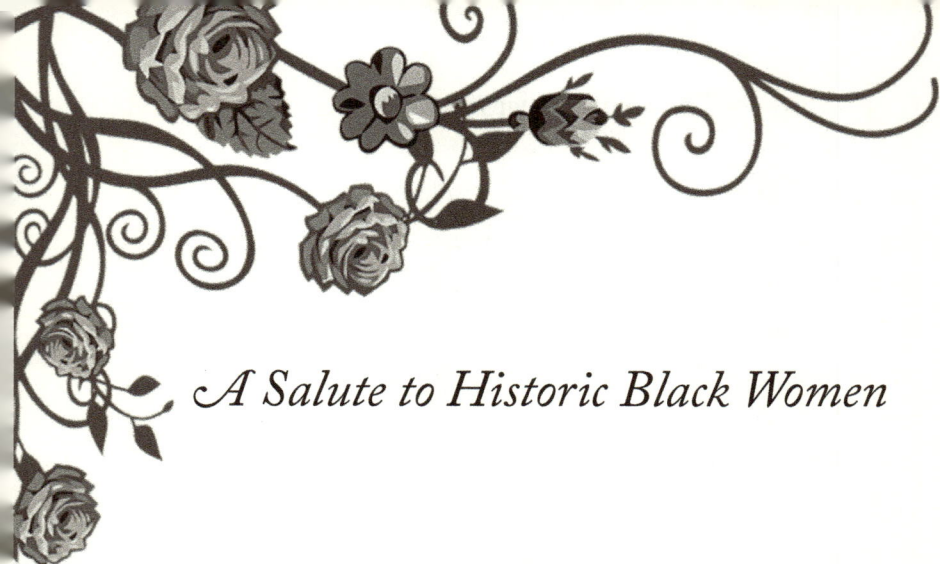

A Salute to Historic Black Women

Sojourner Truth, **Madame Walker** and **Harriett Tubman** were the most talked about historic women.

1753—1784 Phillis Wheatley the first Black female poetess in the United States of America.

On an ordinary day in 1761, a ship docked in Boston harbor bearing a most precious cargo. Somewhere buried in its hull was a little slave girl of unknown origin. Some say she was from Ethiopia; others say Bengal, West Africa; judging from the loss of her first teeth. She became a pioneer in literary history, a poetess of the American Revolution and first Black female poetess in the United States. She married a pseudo-gentleman; he was not a good provider and she was forced to work as a servant. She gave birth to three children; the children died and she died shortly after the children. She wrote a poem Dec 5, 1784 just before she died entitled "Liberty and Peace."

1867—1919 Madame C. J. Walker was America's first Black millionaire business woman. She achieved her success by discovering a new hair care process and marketing a line of toilet articles and cosmetics for Black women. Madame Walker died on May 25, 1919. At the time of her death she had acquired a vast empire of one million dollars. Among real estate holdings (left to her daughter) was a $250,000 30-room mansion Villa Lewaro built in New York in 1917. There were many other facts about Madame Walker that may not have been written in many books.

1797—1883 Sojourner Truth. Born Isabella Baumfree was a pilgrim of freedom and a fervent women's rights activist. Truth was the first Black woman orator to lecture against slavery. How she became Sojourner Truth, she asked the Lord to give her a new name because she was to travel the land wearing a satin banner across her chest showing people their sins and being a sign unto them. She asked the Lord for a last name and he gave her Truth—Sojourner Truth. The highlight of her life was when she was received by President Lincoln at the White House. Her epitaph is taken from a well-known retort she once made to Frederick Douglass, her speech was regarding the plight of Black Americans, and Sojourner rose and asked, "Frederick is God dead?" This woman who could neither read or write, when she spoke, crowds flocked to hear her. There is a great story about her life; you ought to look it up.

1893—1987 Ella Phillips Stewart resided in Toledo, Ohio as a nationally known Black woman pharmacist. She was born to a share cropper in a small town in Berryville, Virginia in 1893. She was inducted into the Hall of Fame in 1948, she was elected to four-year term as president of the National Association of Colored Woman (NACW) and authorized a book (Lifting as They Climbed in 1951), and the City of Toledo named a $3 million elementary school after her. Ella Phillip Stewart was acclaimed as a Black woman. She is further distinguished as having been the oldest living Black female pharmacist in the United States at the time of her death.

1887—1933 Florence Beatrice Smith Price was the first Black woman to be recognized as an award winning composer. She was born on April 9, 1887 in Little Rock Arkansas. Her mother, a music teacher, recognized her musical talent and taught her to play the piano at an early age. She gave her first recital at the age of four. Florence Price left behind a musical repertoire classed among the best. She died in Chicago on June 3, 1933, but not before establishing herself as a worthy, creative Black American.

1912—1967 Nina Mae McKinney was the first Black female motion picture star. She was named "one of the most beautiful women of her time." Although her career did not soar, her initial portrayal of the sultry "chick" became the standard for enticing leading ladies in the motion picture industry. She died in 1967.

1893—1926 Bessie Coleman received her air pilot's license in 1923 from Federation Aeronautique International in France to become the first Black woman pilot. Her life ended when her plane crashed. It is said that every year on Memorial Day, pilots fly over Bessie Coleman's grave and drop flowers in her honor.

1875—1955 Mary Jane McLeod Bethune was the first Black woman in the United States to establish a school that became a four-year accredited college. She was born to slave parents. She was champion of human rights, a woman beloved by all regardless of race, color or creed. In 1995, she closed her eyes for the last time.

1862—1931 Ida B. Wells Barnett, co-founder of the NAACP, an anti-lynch crusader and a most courageous Black woman journalist. She was born of slaves in Holly Spring, Mississippi in 1862. In 1891, she taught segregated public school in Memphis, Tennessee from 1881 to 1891. She wrote articles for *Free Speech*, a black newspaper. In 1891, the Memphis Board of Education fired her because her articles were fiery and controversial. Mrs. Barnett was cited as one of the 25 outstanding women in Chicago's history. One of the housing projects bears her name. She died in 1931.

1839—1867 Mary Elizabeth Bowser served as a union spy. Many accounts of her life were veiled in mystery. Details of her birth and death are unknown. She was born as a slave of John and Elizabeth VanLew. In 1851, Mrs. VanLew freed Mary and other slaves. As a favorite slave, Mary was sent to attend a school in Philadelphia. Accounts of Mary Elizabeth Bowser's war efforts as an espionage agent were carefully hidden by Mrs. VanLew even after the war. A secret diary was buried in Mrs. VanLew's yard. Certain pages relating to Mary's activities had been ripped out by Mrs. VanLew in order to protect Mary from any reprisal.

1826—1897 Ellen Craft was noted as a "master of disguise." Because of her nearly white complexion, she was able to 'pass' and with the help of her husband, ingeniously escaped from slavery, she as a respectable white gentleman and he as 'his' slave. Ellen was born in Clinton, Georgia, the daughter of her White master. She was often mistakenly taken for a member of the family. When she was 11 years old, she was taken from her mother and given to her owner's daughter as a "wedding present" although Ellen was a favorite slave. She died in 1891 and her husband died in 1900.

1867—1953 Dr. Ida Gray Nelson became the first Black woman in America's history to earn a Doctor of Dental Surgery degree. Dr. Gray was born in Clarksville, Tennessee in 1867. It was said she was so good that a newspaper editor said of Dr. Gray "her blushing winning way makes you feel like finding an extra tooth anyway to allow her to pull."

1893—1965 Crystal Dreda Bird Fauset was a race relations specialist and the first Black woman state legislator. In 1918, she traveled the country as field secretary for the YWCA. She developed programs for Black working students. She made 200 speeches and reached more than 50,000 people in a single year. She helped establish the Swarthmore College Institute of Race Relations. In 1935 she assisted the Director of the

Philadelphia Workers Program Administration (W.P.A.). She served also in organizing as Director of Colored Women Activities for the Democratic National Committee. In 1939 she became the first woman in history to be given a seat on the United States House of Representatives. In 1945, she founded the United States Council of Philadelphia which later became the World Affairs Council. She died in her sleep on March 28, 1965.

1814—1904 Mary Ellen Pleasant was noted as a financial genius and the mother of the civil rights struggle in California. She died in 1904 and left an estate of $300,000 to those who cared for her in her declining years.

1848—1918 Dr. Susan McKinney Steward is the first Black woman to formally enter the medical profession to gain recognizable success. She practiced for many years. She died in 1918.

1820—1913 Harriet Ross Tubman—Strong as a man, brave as a lion, cunning as a fox. She was one of the greatest Underground Railroad conductors of her time.

As I was about to end my writing, I was sitting at the kitchen table, where I sit most of the time when I have a moment to sit. When you live alone in a house, there is more to do than one individual can master. I turned on the television to listen to the news and was shocked to see a young high school boy being handcuffed and taken into custody because he had just shot and killed ten people in the classroom, including two teachers, in Texas. That was a repeat of what had happened in the State of Florida. It was almost too much to look at and too much to not look at. It was like a nightmare. But I knew that it was real so as I was watching, uncontrollable tears began streaming down my face. I had traveled to the state of Florida only once and never to Texas and didn't know anything about the schools there in either state. But I couldn't have been more emotional than if I had known them because they were all given life by Almighty God.

I don't know whether either of those young boys had ever been taught, or heard about God Almighty, or our Lord and Savior Jesus Christ, or about our adversary the Devil who walks up and down daily seeking whom he may devour. From the minute a soul is born into this world, there is an undeveloped spirit of right and wrong within the heart.

My granddaughter Brandy gave birth to her first child at the age of forty-two and the baby turned one-year-old a month ago. I asked her if the baby had learned to walk and she laughed and said "Grandma, she is running, especially when she does things that she knows she shouldn't and sees me looking at her, she runs." I believe that every person is born with a spirit. The way the spirit is developed, nurtured, and trained from early childhood has a tremendous impact on the life of an individual. A child's life is also impacted by the situations and circumstances that he/she is exposed to early in life.

I wish that every parent would take the time to teach their children about life, their salvation, and who gives life to all. In these days it seems that everyone does what they feel is right for them. We need to remember that the ways of the Lord are right; the righteous will walk in them but the rebellious will stumble in them. God is slow to anger, abounding in love and faithfulness, bestowing love upon thousands and forgiving wickedness, rebellion and sin to those who repent. Yet he does not leave the guilty unpunished. He is willing to forgive but also ready to punish.

The prayer we commonly teach our children is:

"Now I lay me down to sleep,
I pray to the Lord my soul to keep
If I should die before I wake
I pray to the Lord my soul to take."

When this prayer is taught, it should be made clear to the children what is meant by sleep and the Lord taking your soul. There are many people who know a lot of words, but never know what they really mean. As they get older, they are taught the prayer that the Lord taught His disciples to pray:

"Our Father who art in heaven, Hallowed be thy name, thy kingdom come. Thy will be done on earth as it is in heaven. Give us this day our daily bread and forgive us our trespasses as we forgive those who trespass against us. Lead us not into temptation but deliver us from evil for thine is the kingdom and the power and the glory forever. Amen."

They should be taught that God is our father, and how do we hallow His name and what it means about thy kingdom, what the kingdom is how does it come, and where.

- What the will of God is and how we can do it?
- What is our daily bread?
- What forgiveness is and what trespasses are?
- What temptation is and what evil is?
- Thine is the kingdom, where and what is God's kingdom, what is power and what is glory?
- What does Amen mean?
- What does the house of God mean?
- Who God is and the reason that we go to Heaven?
- What does salvation mean?
- How does or can one be saved from our sins?
- What is sin?

Salvation and Baptism

One of the most important Scriptures in the Bible is Romans 10:9-10: "That if you confess with your mouth the Lord Jesus and believe in your heart that God has raised Him from the dead, you will be saved. [10] For with the heart one believes unto righteousness and with the mouth confession is made unto salvation." The process of being saved is very simple. It's a good thing when someone leads another person to the Lord. But you can receive Jesus as your savior all by yourself. Just believe the verses that I just quoted above (Romans 10:9-10) In other words, believe that Jesus died to pay for your sins and that God raised Him from the dead, and accept it and say it out loud, for example, say "Jesus I accept you as my Savior," or tell someone, "I'm a Christian." It's that simple to change the destination of where you will spend eternity. Do you know of anything else that is so valuable and can be acquired so easily?

Baptism is a symbol of the death, burial and resurrection of our Savior Jesus Christ. To be called a Christian means that you are buried with Him, died to sin and being brought up out of the water, a changed person to walk in the newness of life, living as Jesus commanded, following the path of righteousness, and not doing the wrong thing.

I pray that parents, or someone in the church will teach all young church members the doctrine of the church so they can understand the church's methods and principles. I hope young people come to understand the benefits of the Kingdom of God, as well as they understand the benefits of secular principles and benefits, such as getting a good education and a good job. Those things are temporary, but the Kingdom of God is eternal.

I believe when people know and understand why they do what they do, they will take more responsibility and be more committed to what they do in Church.

Parents are very important people on this planet earth, the way they live and what they do and teach impact the life and well-being of their children and their children's children. Both good and evil, safety and destruction rests in the hands of man. (Genesis 1:27, 28-2:18) God gave man a help meet and allowed them to be mothers and fathers of precious beautiful children to be brought in the world. So why would parents trust their little ones into the hands of the media, videos, phones and Facebook. So parents, what are your kids watching? Do you know the impact social media has on their lives? To take a stand is to turn your children away from the manipulation and babble of the mass media that so easily distracts them and tempts them to go down a path that is contrary to the Word of God. The Bible tells us "the eye never has enough of seeing nor the ear its fill of hearing:" Eccl 1:8 NIV). The modern media works upon those senses that are more susceptible to distraction.

Guns and Roses

Researchers say MTV, the marriage between television and music is especially destructive. The book "Dancing in the Dark" calls MTV one of the most powerful forms of contemporary propaganda."

As music affects behavior, it affects our moods, our attitudes, our emotions and our behavior. Research found that the average teenager listens to rock music four to six hours each day but nothing is said about how many teenagers are now singing in church choirs. As a matter of fact, there is not much said about church choir singing period, except that which is written on a church service bulletin, or the Sunday morning program.

Popular music is not without its many negative anecdotes. Examples of copycat crimes, such as:

- Suicide solution
- Devil-worshipping
- Aggressive rebellion
- Abuse of drugs and alcohol

- Graphic violence and suicide
- Fascination with the occult
- Sexuality that is graphic and explicit
- Partying
- Loud music
- Disrespect—foul language, heretical
- Anger
- Jealousy

These things are becoming more popular among Christian world leaders as well as non-Christians. I pray that whatever your local church cultural association or denomination has adopted, that we understand that we are called to develop the discernment to know right from wrong, the wisdom to see what is right, the knowledge to pursue what is right, and the understanding to persevere. We must be mindful of the fact that, "God has not given us a spirit of fear but of power and love and of sound mind." (2 Timothy 1:7 KJV)

Pay Attention

The time in which we live has become a spin down, where things that we once thought was so far away are really very close. And so it is with end of life. Our time is so much closer than we once thought. Sometimes we spend so much time looking at others and what they are doing and forget about ourselves.

Some people are so busy watching others that it causes them to become so desensitized and confused that they become copycats. It is true that children learn, to a large degree, by mimicking the behavior of the adults around them including those on televisions and in movies.

(NOTE) Whenever there are books, videos, tapes, records even some toys advertised for children, parents need to check them out before giving them to their children. Television can have a negative influence on young minds. MTV's series Beavis and Butthead was blamed for giving a five-year-old the idea to set a fire in his home that killed his two-year-old sister. I have observed people watching violent scenes on TV and sometimes just enjoying sports, their facial expressions shows the emotional changes (frown, smile, laughter or cheer etc.) as long as the one that they care about wins. (I John 2:15 Do not love the world or the things in the world." If anyone loves the world, the love of the father is not in Him; (2:16) for all that is in the world, the lust of the flesh, the lust of the eyes and the pride of life is not of the father but of the world.)

Take Every Thought Captive

Taking our thought captive is a must for today's Christian family. We must be concerned about the media's impact on us, our children, and our community. We as Christians are called to be salt and light in our home, Church, community and workplace. Parents must pay attention to who their children associate with. There are many seducing spirits out there that might entice your child:

Pay attention to the words you say in the presence of your children.

Pay attention to the Gospel message, don't ignore it because, our nation needs healing. We need to understand the message that God is sending and apply it to our lives daily.

Pay attention to elderly parents; Get involved in their everyday living and their business so that you will know what to do when it's time for you to step up to the plate.

- Know about their finances
- Know what bills they owe
- Know who is their primary doctor

- Know what medicines they take
- Know where their medicines are kept
- Know where all their business papers are kept
- Know where their clothes, esp. gowns and under clothes are
- Know what kind of foods are kept and check expiration dates
- Know who their friends, neighbors, pastor and church friends are
- Know where their written Will is
- Consider the status of elderly parents
- Pass these things on to your children

Pay attention: The biblical foundation of our society is cracking. Disaster looms in front of us. Yet in spite of the clear correlation between violence in our homes, and on the streets, very few people are coming together in our churches and community to pray and come up with interventional programs or projects to help change the course of our young people.

The tolerance for brutal sex and violence, gun packing, drugs and gangs are running rampant in our streets, especially in the Black communities. Churches are holding fewer services, fewer males are attending and/or participating in the worship services. Youth choirs, and young women's circles are almost obsolete in the church; senior choirs have disrobed themselves as a symbol of unity in most of the churches. Some Church members claim that they cannot afford to buy choir robes or uniforms due to the economic situation, yet they are making the Chinese richer buying hair, beads, bows and every other beautiful items that they market. Blacks are afraid to open a beauty supply store, small restaurant, gas station, or any other business, how pitiful!

The following Scripture from Paul's letters to the Romans describe the condition in which we find ourselves today. "And even as they did not like to retain God in their knowledge, God gave them over to reprobate mind...." (Romans 1:28)

I am sure that most people pay attention to our capitol (Washington, DC) and the news media near and far. I wonder how many take captive what they see and hear and whether they can distinguish between the good and the bad. Will they accept those leaders to lead this country or will every man turn to his own way? The language that is communicated over national TV from our leaders of the country is the same as what we hear on the street and from prison inmates. Some of those on the street haven't had any teaching or training, don't have any money or a home of their own to live in, and some simply don't care about themselves or anyone else. So what makes us think that those who are highly educated are better than those who don't have much education and don't desire to have any if they speak the same language and do same things?

With all the violence, and corruption and destruction that we see in our world today, why aren't the pastors, ministers or evangelists being called upon to speak the gospel of Jesus Christ to these suffering people? The lack of presenting a Christian world view gospel makes the Church and the

Christian faith seem irrelevant to young people. The Church was originally the dominant force in building our schools, hospitals, and producing scholarly statesmen who drafted state constitutions, federal constitution, and charitable organizations that provide care for the poor and widows.

The agenda for today's public square is clearly shaped by secular and anti-Christian forces. To young men and women who are thinking about living rather than dying, this makes the church appear unimportant.

Some church critics, according to a writing by Ted Baehr of the media-wise family, says that ministers would be more influential if they would speak out on the conditions and problems that suppress the people in the community, rather than just teaching people how to get to heaven.

I believe that if everyone would find their God-given purposes and strive to fulfill that purpose, they would be connected to the power of God and influence their generation for the Kingdom of God. I believe that it should be most desirable for all believers to strive for heaven, and try to take as many as they can with them. Hebrews 9:27 (KJV) says "And as it is appointed unto men once to die, but after this the judgment." I think if people were taught the consequences of the things they do, their choices would be different.

Conclusion

I want people to know that life isn't just a bed of roses. I also want you to know that life is worth living. I am thankful for all the beauty of God's handiwork that has been displayed here on this planet earth. My experiences here and God's provision and the blessed hope in Jesus Christ that I look forward to will by far exceed all that I have encountered here on the earth because I definitely believe that His Holy Bible is true. I truly thank God for parents who taught and showed me the true way.

I trust that those of you who took the time to read this book will find something that will be inspiring and encouraging to you as you continue to embark upon life's trail. As you live through some of life's unpleasant experience, that you come to realize that you are not alone and remember that only what we do for Christ will last and be counted.

I thank God for the precious gifts, knowledge, and talents that He has given me, and allowed my family to use to help themselves and to help many others. Most of our families were home owners at the beginning of their adult lives, and independence and business ownership is a family culture that is now being passed on to the next generation. Most of all, I thank God that most of my family members have confessed the Lord Jesus Christ as Savior. That supersedes anything else they, you, or anyone else can ever accomplish here on this earth.

Thank you Lord Jesus!